SANTA MONICA PUBLIC LIBRARY
I SMP 00 2410388 B
DISCARD
W9-CEK-404
FAIRVIEW BRANCH
Santa Monica Public Library
JUL 2014

EYEWITNESS

ROCKS & MINERALS

Slice from septarian nodule
Garnet-chlorite schist
Gypsum desert rose
Cinnabar
Hematite
Granite
Wenlock limestone with triolobite fossils

Opal

Cut tourmalines

EYEWITNESS

ROCKS & MINERALS

Written by
Dr. R. F. SYMES

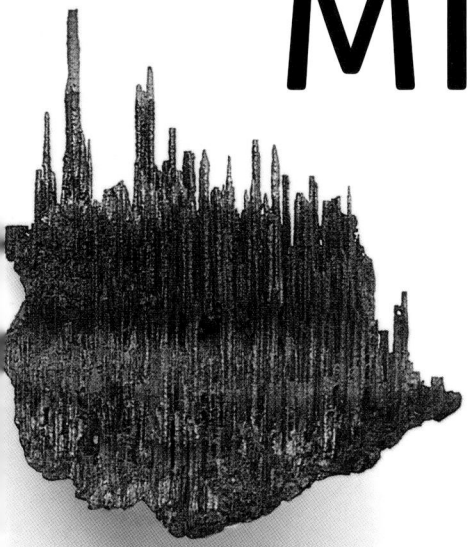

Geothite

Pyrite

Obsidian

Sulfur

Nephrite "tiki"

Labradorite

DK

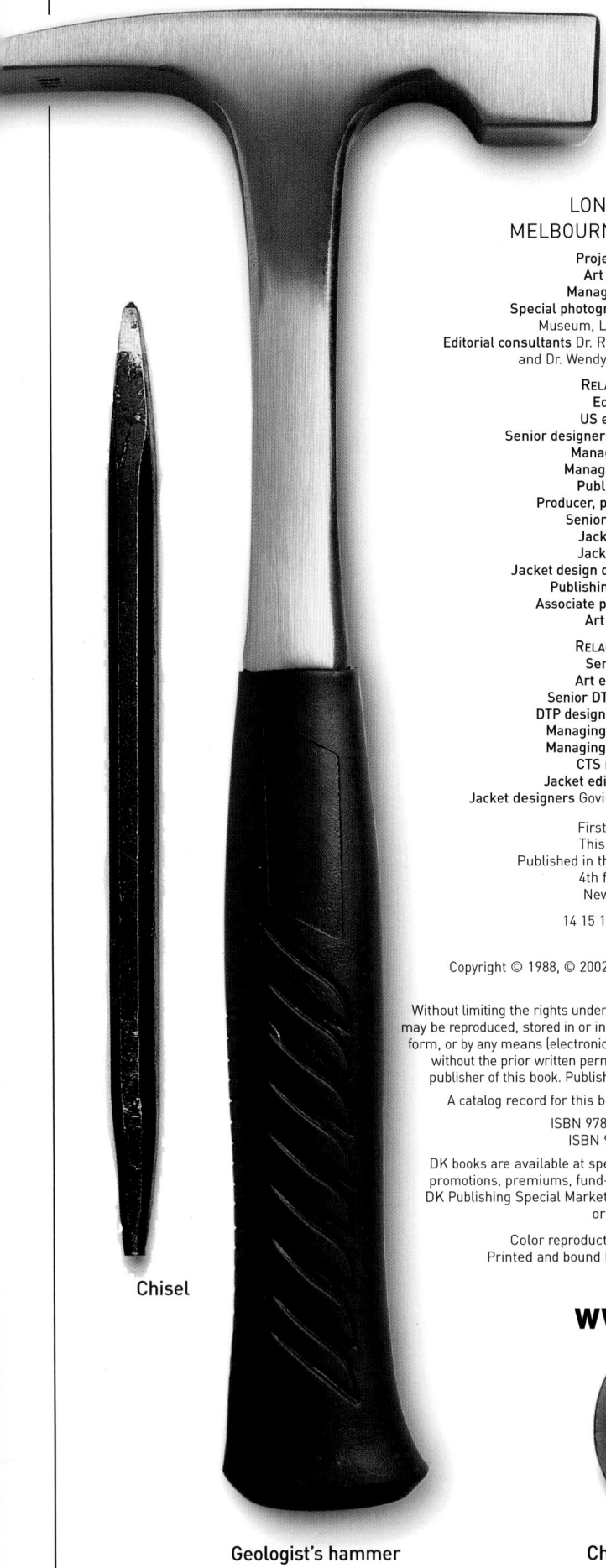

Chisel

Geologist's hammer

Magnifying lens

Mixed rough and polished pebbles

Chalcedony cameo

LONDON, NEW YORK,
MELBOURNE, MUNICH, AND DELHI

Project editor Janice Lacock
Art editor Neville Graham
Managing art editor Jane Owen
Special photography Colin Keates (Natual History Museum, London) and Andreas Einsiedel
Editorial consultants Dr. R. F. Symes (Natural History Museum, London) and Dr. Wendy Kirk (University College London)

Relaunch Edition (DK UK)
Editor Ashwin Khurana
US editor Margaret Parrish
Senior designers Rachael Grady, Spencer Holbrook
Managing editor Gareth Jones
Managing art editor Philip Letsu
Publisher Andrew Macintyre
Producer, preproduction Adam Stoneham
Senior producer Charlotte Cade
Jacket editor Maud Whatley
Jacket designer Laura Brim
Jacket design development manager Sophia MTT
Publishing director Jonathan Metcalf
Associate publishing director Liz Wheeler
Art director Phil Ormerod

Relaunch Edition (DK India)
Senior editor Neha Gupta
Art editor Deep Shikha Walia
Senior DTP designer Harish Aggarwal
DTP designers Anita Yadav, Pawan Kumar
Managing editor Alka Thakur Hazarika
Managing art editor Romi Chakraborty
CTS manager Balwant Singh
Jacket editorial manager Saloni Talwar
Jacket designers Govind Mittal, Suhita Dharamjit, Vidit Vashisht

First American Edition, 1988
This American Edition, 2014
Published in the United States by DK Publishing
4th floor, 345 Hudson Street
New York, New York 10014

14 15 16 17 18 10 9 8 7 6 5 4 3 2 1
196434—07/14

Copyright © 1988, © 2002, © 2007, © 2014 Dorling Kindersley Limited
All rights reserved

Without limiting the rights under copyright reserved above, no part of this publication may be reproduced, stored in or introduced into a retrieval system, or transmitted, in any form, or by any means (electronic, mechanical, photocopying, recording, or otherwise), without the prior written permission of both the copyright owner and the above publisher of this book. Published in Great Britain by Dorling Kindersley Limited.

A catalog record for this book is available from the Library of Congress.

ISBN 978-1-4654-2056-5 (Paperback)
ISBN 978-1-4654- 2098-5 (ALB)

DK books are available at special discounts when purchased in bulk for sales promotions, premiums, fund-raising, or educational use. For details, contact: DK Publishing Special Markets, 345 Hudson Street, New York, New York 10014 or SpecialSale@dk.com.

Color reproduction by Alta Image Ltd., London, UK
Printed and bound by South China Printing Co. Ltd., China

Discover more at
www.dk.com

Contents

Earth 6
Rocks and their minerals 8
How rocks are formed 10
Weathering and erosion 12
Rocks on the seashore 14
Igneous rock 16
Volcanic rock 18
Sedimentary rock 20
Limestone 22
Metamorphism 24
Marble 26
The first flint tools 28
Rocks as tools 30
Pigments 32
Building stones 34
The story of coal 36
Fossils 38
Space rocks 40
Minerals 42
Crystals 44
Crystal growth 46
The properties of minerals 48
Gemstones 50
Decorative stones 52
Other gems 54
Ore minerals 56
Precious metals 58
Cutting and polishing 60
Starting a collection 62
Did you know? 64
Rock or mineral? 66
Find out more 68
Glossary 70
Index 72

Earth

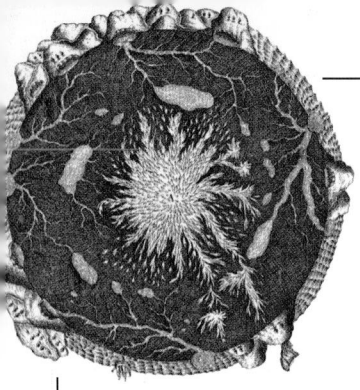

Early view of Earth with a central fire

One of eight planets that revolve around the Sun, Earth is thought to be about 4.6 billion years old.

The word geology comes from the ancient Greek for Earth and study. The many different types of rocks found on our planet hold valuable details about Earth's long history, so geologists study them and figure out the processes and events that produced them.

Seashore pebbles
These are formed by the weathering of larger rocks by wave action.

Precious metals
Platinum, silver, and gold are valuable, rare metals.

Gold in quartz vein

Crystal habits
The shape of a crystal is known as its habit.

Cubes of pyrite

Mineral ores
These are the source of most useful metals.

Cut citrine, a variety of quartz

Cassiterite, tin ore, from Bolivia

Diamond in kimberlite

Gemstones
Rare, hard-wearing, and attractive minerals may be cut as gemstones, mainly for jewelry.

Quartz crystals from France

Crystals
Many minerals form regular-shaped solids with flat surfaces, known as crystals.

Shell limestone

Fossils
These rocks contain the remains of, or impressions made by, former plants or animals.

Earth's structure
Earth consists of a core, mantle, and crust. The crust and upper mantle form vast plates that move slowly over the mantle beneath. The closer to the Earth's center, the greater the temperature and pressure.

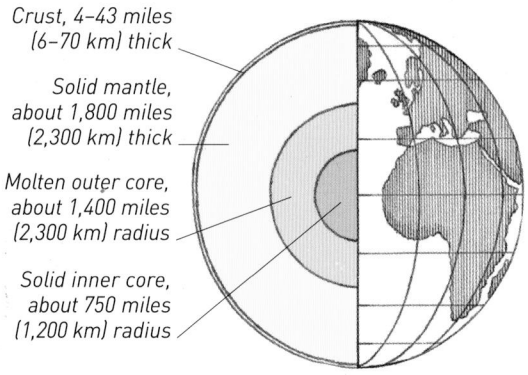

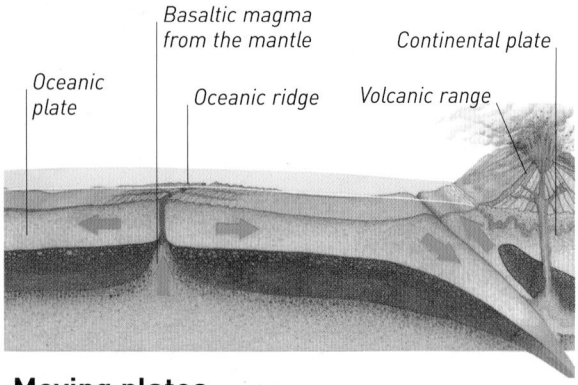

Moving plates
Where plates collide, mountain ranges may form. Where they pull apart, magma rises to form deep-sea ridges. When one sinks beneath another, volcanoes erupt.

Quartzite beach pebbles

Igneous rocks

The most common types of rock have formed from molten magma.

Granite

Satellite image of Nile River

Egypt's Nile River carries debris eroded from rocks and deposits it in the delta and sea, where it may slowly form sedimentary rocks.

Volcanic rocks

Volcanic activity produces a number of different types of rock and lava.

Hawaiian ropy lava

Carboniferous limestone

Sedimentary rocks

These rocks are formed by the accumulation and compaction of loose sediments that have built up in layers.

Anthracite, the hardest form of coal

Coal

One type of sedimentary rock, coal has formed from the fossilized remains of prehistoric plants.

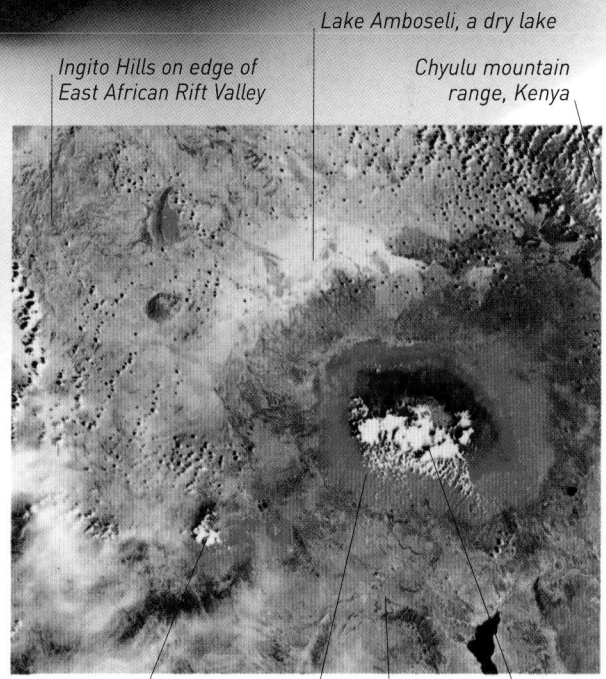

Landsat image of East Africa

This area shows a range of landscapes, formed from different rocks, such as volcanic rocks forming volcanic Mount Kilimanjaro, and evaporites in dried-up lakes.

Rocks and their minerals

James Hutton (1726– 1797), one of the founders of modern geology

Rocks are natural aggregates or combinations of one or more minerals. Some rocks contain only one mineral, but most consist of more. Minerals are inorganic solids with definite chemical compositions and an ordered atomic arrangement. Here, two common rocks—granite and basalt—are shown with specimens of the major minerals of which they are formed.

Granite and its major minerals
Minerals' size and texture vary with how a rock forms. In the coarse-grained rock, granite, the major minerals are visible to the naked eye: quartz (1); mica (2); feldspar (3).

Basalt and its major minerals
The main minerals in basalt are olivine (1), plagioclase feldspar (2), and pyroxene (3). Since it is fine-grained, it is not always possible to distinguish them with the naked eye. This olivine basalt was collected from a volcano in Hawaii.

1 Olivine
Transparent green crystals of olivine are very rare and known as peridot.

2 Feldspar
Flat or polished crystals of labradorite (a plagioclase feldspar) display beautiful colors.

1 Quartz
These quartz crystals have milky, etched faces.

2 Mica
Black biotite (a form of mica) crystals can be split into thin sheets.

3 Feldspar
Crystals of orthoclase (a feldspar) are pale pink or milky white.

3 Pyroxene
This well developed, single black crystal of augite (a pyroxene) comes from Italy. Augite crystals are found in various igneous rocks.

)iverse forms

ɔcks are not always ɜrd and resistant— ose sand and wet ay are considered be rocks. The dividual size minerals in rock ranges from nall specks, in a ıe-grained volcanic ɔck, to many yards a granite pegmatite.

Rocks formed within rocks
This sedimentary rock specimen is a claystone septarian nodule. Nodules such as this form when groundwater redistributes minerals within a rock in a particular nodular pattern. Here, the pattern of veins is formed of calcite.

rystals of ore mineral
ange-red tabular crystals of ılfenite form in lead- and olybdenum-bearing ore veins.

Eruption of Mount Pelée, Martinique, on August 5, 1851

Rocks from volcanic eruption
"Pele's hair" consists of golden-brown, hairlike fibers of basalt glass, which occasionally enclose minute olivine crystals. It was formed from the eruption of basaltic magma as a lava spray.

Rocks formed by evaporation
Stalactites are substances deposited when dripping water evaporates. This blue-green stalactite of the mineral chalcanthite (copper sulfate) was formed from percolating copper-rich waters in a mine.

Section of a mine roof colored with deposits of the copper mineral, chalcanthite

Rocks that form in layers
Norite is an igneous rock made of the minerals pyroxene, plagioclase feldspar, and chromite. In this specimen, the dark and light minerals have separated into layers. The dark chromite layers constitute an important source of chromium.

How rocks are formed

Geological processes work in continual cycles, redistributing chemical elements, minerals, and rocks. These processes are driven by the Earth's internal heat and, at its surface, by the Sun's energy.

Andesite formed from a volcanic eruption in the Solomon Islands in the Pacific

Pure quartz sand formed from weathered granites o sandstone

Volcanic activity

When rocks of the crust and upper mantle melt, they form magma, which volcanic activity brings to Earth's surface as extrusive igneous rocks. Basalt is the most common.

Basaltic lava from Hawaii

Survivor

Le Puy de Dôme, France, is the plug once at the core of an ancient volcano.

Igneous inselberg

Sugar Loaf Mountain, Brazil, consists of intrusive igneous rocks exposed by weathering.

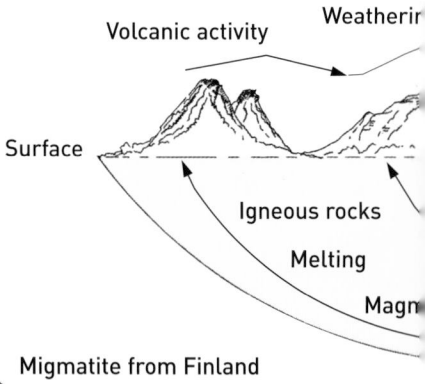

Gabbro, a basalt, from Finland

Feldspar crystal

Granite containing feldspar crystals, from England

Migmatite from Finland

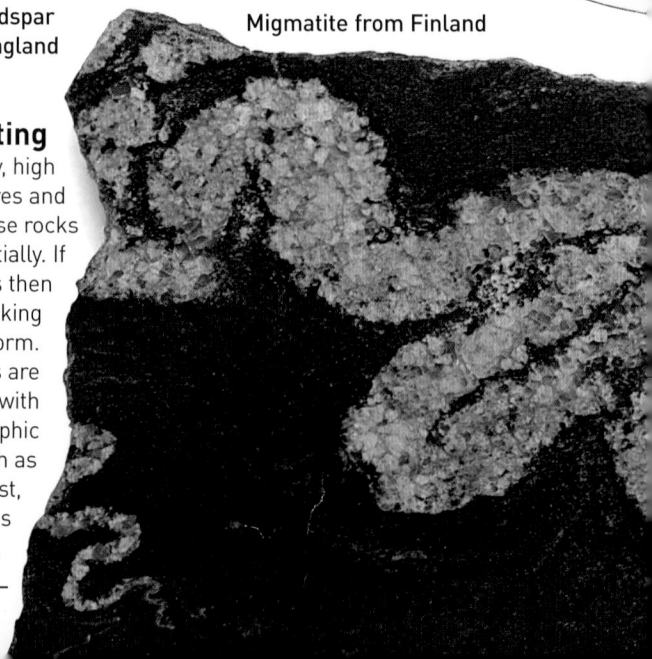

Rocks from magma

Rocks formed within Earth from molten magma are called intrusive igneous rocks. Those that cooled slowly, deep under the surface (such as granite), are called plutonic, after Pluto, the Greek god of the underworld.

Melting

Occasionally, high temperatures and pressures cause rocks to melt partially. If the rock is then squeezed, snaking veins may form. Migmatites are mixed rocks with a metamorphic host, such as gneiss or schist, cut by veins of granite.

'eathering

; wind, rain, ice, and heat act on rocks, ey may may lead to chemical changes cause the rocks to fragment and form diments, such as sand grains and clays.

Clays produced by weathering become important components of soils

Deposition of sediments

Sediments are transported by rivers, or by the wind in desert regions, and eventually deposited into layers of different-sized particles. When compacted, the layers form sedimentary rocks.

Layered sandstone from the US

River transportation

Rivers such as these (seen from space) transport rock debris from one area to another. Each day, the Mississippi deposits thousands of tons of debris into its delta.

Banded claystone from Uganda

Desert sandstone from Scotland that is 200-million-year-old

'he rock cycle

here is no starting point this cycle, which has been oing on for millions of years.

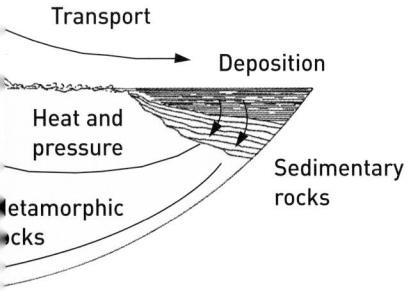

Metamorphic rocks

Quartz veins stand out in this schist rock face in Scotland, an area that is rich in metamorphic rocks.

Quartzite, an altered sandstone, formed by pressure and heat

Gneiss, a banded metamorphic rock

Mica schist formed from metamorphosed claystones

Metamorphism

The deeper a rock is within Earth, the greater the pressure exerted on it from the overlying rocks, and the higher the temperature. Pressure and heat cause the rocks to change or "metamorphose" as the minerals recrystallize. The new rocks (such as gneiss, mica, and quartzite, above) are termed metamorphic rocks.

Weathering and erosion

Rocks at the Earth's surface all break down. Weathering, chemical or mechanical, breaks them down as they stand. Erosion breaks them down further as they are moved, by the action of water, ice, or wind.

Wind erosion

Sediment-laden wind may slowly grind away at a rock.

Monument Valley, US
Abrasion by the wind produces large, protruding "buttes."

Abrasion by the wind
Softer layers of rock are worn away, leaving the harder ones protruding.

Sand blasting
Faceted sand-blown desert pebbles are called "dreikanters."

Weathering caused by temperature

The expansion and contraction of rock as the temperature varies causes it to break up. Water expanding in the rock as it freezes can cause frost-shattering.

Sandstone composed of sand accumulated 200 million years ago in a desert environment

Sand from a present-day desert in Saudi Arabia

Desert erosion
In deserts, where sediment is carried by wind, rocks are often reddish and composed of rounded sand grains.

Desert environment
Wind and temperature changes cause continual weathering and barren landscapes in the Sahara Desert.

Onion-skin weathering
Changes in temperature cause the surface layers of rock to expand, contract, and peel away.

Fine-graine doleri

Onion-ski weathere doleri

Peeling layers like onion skin expose the underlying rock

hemical veathering

inerals dissolved acidic rainwater the surface may e carried down into e soil and rock below.

Fresh, unaltered granite (left)

Coarse, weathered granite

Altered minerals
Granite is split as water freezes and expands. Its chemically altered minerals form coarse rock.

Granite tors, UK
Tors are weathered, rounded rocks left when surrounding rock has been eroded away.

Rock altered by ercolating groundwater

Secondary minerals

Chemical changes
These brightly colored "secondary minerals" were formed from deposits of dissolved minerals from weathered rocks higher up.

Tropical weathering
In the tropics, quartz is dissolved and carried off, while feldspars are altered to clay minerals that may form a surface deposit of bauxite.

arthenon, Athens, Greece
hemicals in the air can react with stone d cause weathering of monuments.

Ice erosion

As glaciers move they pick up fragments of rock, which form part of its icy base. The moving, frozen mass causes further erosion of underlying rocks.

Scratched rock
This limestone from Grindelwald, Switzerland, was gouged by fragments of rock in the glacier that flowed over it.

Swiss glacier
Glaciers are a major cause of erosion in mountainous regions.

Glacier deposits
A till is a deposit left by a melting glacier and contains crushed rock fragments. Ancient tills formed into hard rock are called "tillite." This specimen is from the Flinders Ranges in South Australia, which was glaciated some 600 million years ago.

Rocks on the seashore

Many seashores are backed by cliffs. Coarse material that has fallen from above is gradually broken up by the sea and sorted into pebbles, gravel, sand, and mud. These various sizes are then deposited separately—the raw material for future sedimentary rocks.

Pebbles on Chesil Beach, England

Graded grains
On the beach, these pebbles are sorted by waves and tides. The sand is pure quartz—other minerals were washed away.

Large, coarse pebbles

Irregularly shaped pyrite nodule

Mica schist

Slates

Skimming stones
The best skimming stones are disk-shaped and are probably sedimentary or metamorphic rocks, as they split into sheets.

Local stones
These pebbles are metamorphic rocks that have been worn into flat disks on the beach where they were collected.

Hidden crystals
Pyrite nodules are common in chalk areas. The dull, bumby outside breaks open to reveal glistening crystals inside.

Shell pebbles
Uninhabited sea shells are battered by continuous wave action. In time, the fragments are smoothed into pebbles, like these ones from a beach in New Zealand.

Amber pebbles
Amber is the fossil resin of extinct coniferous trees that lived thousands of years ago. It is especially common along the Baltic coasts of Russia and Poland.

Preserved waves
Visible at low tide, ripple marks form under water from sand carried by currents. This Finnish specimen preserves long-ago ripple marks in sandstone.

lacks sands

areas of volcanic activity, ach sand may be rich in dark nerals. The olivine sand comes m Scotland; the magnetite-aring sand is from Tenerife.

Dark olivine sand

Magnetite-bearing sand

Black volcanic ash beach on north coast of Santorini, Greece

Medium-sized, coarse pebbles

Small, fine pebbles

Finest pebbles

Quartz sand

Marcasite nodule, split in two

Marcasite interior reveals crystals radiating outward

Found in chalk

Because flint nodules are hard, they resist abrasion and may be seen on beaches in chalk areas (right).

White Cliffs of Dover, UK

Granitic origin

In granite country, beach pebbles tend to be of quartz, an abundant vein mineral, or pink or gray granite.

Flint nodules from below chalk cliffs

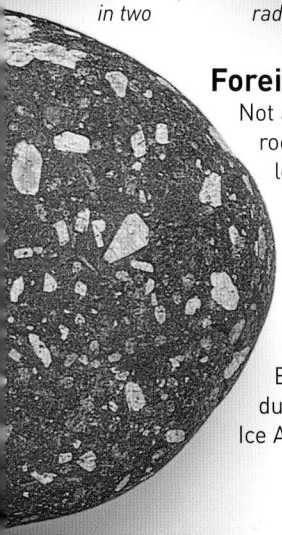

Foreign material

Not all beach rocks are of local derivation. This porphyritic igneous rock was probably carried across the North Sea from Norway to England by ice during the last Ice Age.

Assorted glass pebbles

Brick pebble

Synthetic pebbles

Man-made objects may be washed ashore or dumped on the beach. Some of them may eventually become abraded and rounded by wave action.

Protecting the beach

Artificial groynes stop sand drifting.

Basalt needle, St. Helena

Igneous rock

These rocks form when magma from deep within Earth's crust and upper mantle cools and solidifies. Intrusive ones solidify within the crust and are later exposed by erosion; extrusive ones form when magma erupts as lava and cools.

Giant's Causeway
When basaltic lava cools, it often forms hexagonal columns, as in Northern Irelan

Biotite granite

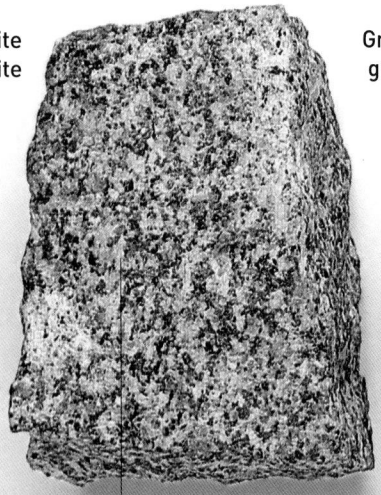

Black grains are biotite, a form of mica

Graphic granite

Long, angular quartz crystals look like ancient writing against the larger, pale-pink feldspar crystals

Red granite

Red coloring due to the high proportion of potassium feldspar in the rock

Granite
An extemely common intrusive rock, granite consists mainly of coarse grains of quartz, feldspar, and mica. The grains are large because they formed as the molten magma cooled slowly deep in the Earth. Generally mottled, granite varies from gray to red according to the different proportions of constituent minerals.

Pitchstone
Formed when volcanic lava cools very quickly, pitchstone contains some crystals of feldspar and quartz, but it has a dull, resinlike appearance and may be brown, black, or gray.

Obsidian
Like pitchstone, obsidian is a glass formed from rapidly cooled lava. It forms so quickly there is no time for crystals to grow. Its characteristically sharp edges made it useful as an early tool.

Feldspar porphyry

Porphyries are rocks that contain large crystals called "phenocrysts" within a medium-grained rock. This particular sample contains feldspar crystals and comes from Wales.

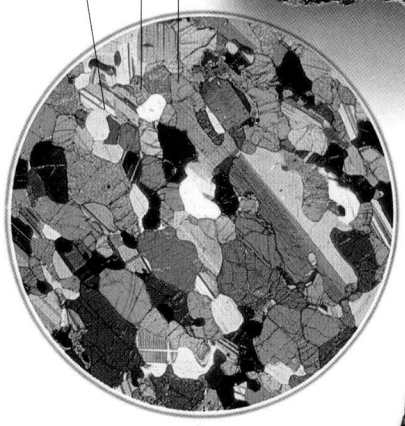

Thin section of gabbro

When a thin slice of rock is seen under a microscope using a certain kind of light, hidden features, such as the crystal shapes of its minerals, appear.

Gabbro

An intrusive rock, gabbro consists of dark minerals such as olivine and augite. It has coarse grains as large crystals formed when the magma slowly cooled.

Basalt

Formed from solidified lava, basalt is the most common extrusive rock. It is similar in composition to gabbro but finer grained. When the lava cools, it may split into many-sided columns, as seen at St. Helena's Needle and Northern Ireland's Giant's Causeway.

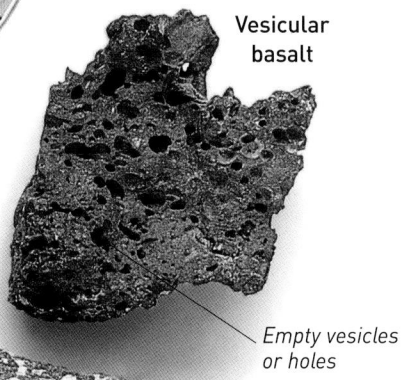

Vesicular volcanic rocks

These two rocks from the volcanically active islands of Hawaii are basalts that were formed when bubbles of gas were trapped in hot lava scum. The vesicular basalt is light and full of holes known as "vesicles." In amygdaloidal basalt, the holes were later filled in with minerals such as calcite.

Peridotite

A dark, heavy rock mainly containing the minerals olivine and pyroxene, peridotite is thought to underlie layers of gabbro 6 miles (10 km) beneath the ocean floor.

Serpentinite

This coarse-grained, red-and-green rock is named after its dominant mineral, serpentine. It is streaked with white veins of calcite. Serpentinite is common in the Alps.

Ejection of lava from Eldfell, Iceland, 1973

Volcanic rock

Rocks formed by volcanic activity can be divided into pyroclastic rocks and acid and basic lavas. The first are formed from either solid rock fragments or "bombs" of lava that solidify as they fly through the air. Acid lavas are thick, sticky, and flow very slowly, forming steep-sided volcanoes. The more fluid, fast-flowing basic lavas spread over vast areas.

Pyroclastic rocks

Pyroclastic rocks consist of rock and lava pieces that were blown apart by exploding gases.

Volcanic bombs

When blobs of lava are thrown out of a volcano, some solidify in the air and land on the ground as hard "bombs." These two specimens are shaped like footballs, but bombs may be spherical or irregular in appearance.

Intrusion breccia formed within a vent

Agglomerate formed close to a vent

Mixed-up pieces

The force of an explosion may cause rocks to fragment. The angular pieces land inside or close to the vent and form rocks known as agglomerates.

Bedded tuff (a hardened ash)

Ash

Inside a volcano

Magma flows through a central vent or side vents. It may form underground dykes that cut across rock layers or sills parallel to them.

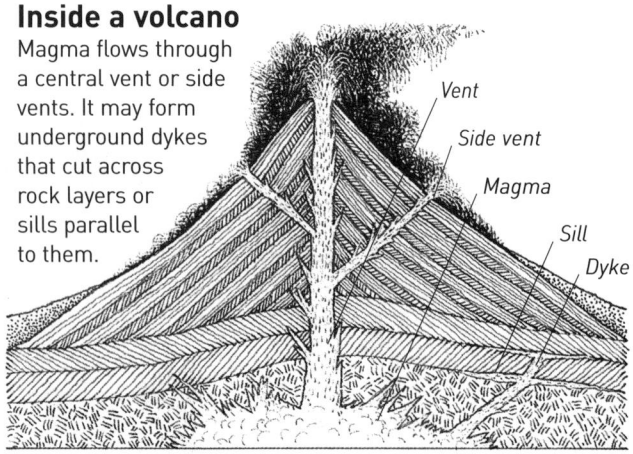

Wind-blown particles

Volcanic ash can travel thousands of miles in the atmosphere. Where it settles and hardens it forms tuff. When Mount St. Helens erupted in 1980, coarse grains were blown 3 miles (5 km); the wind carried fine particles 17 miles (27 km).

Eruption of Mount St. Helens, Washington, 1980

esuvius, 79 CE
is famous eruption produced a
ée ardente, a fast-moving cloud
magma and ash, and destroyed
Roman town of Pompeii.

Aphthitalite

hthitalite

ocks from gases
active volcanoes are "dormant"
volcanic gases may escape
d hot springs form, with
nerals forming rocks like
s one from Vesuvius.

inoan ruins, Santorini
e island blew apart c. 1450 BCE.

Acid lavas

These sticky lavas may solidify in the volcano's vent, trap gases, then explode.

Floating rocks
Pumice is solidified lava froth. Because the froth contains bubbles of gas, the rock is peppered with holes. Pumice is the only rock that floats in water.

Natural glass
Although chemically the same as pumice, obsidian has a totally different, glassy texture. Because it has sharp edges, obsidian was used by primitive man to make tools, arrowheads, and ornaments.

Molasseslike lavas
This light-colored, fine-grained rock is called rhyolite. The distinctive bands formed as the sticky, viscous lava flowed for short distances.

Basic lavas

These lavas flow smoothly, forming flatter volcanoes or welling up through cracks in the ocean floor. As a result, the vent does not get choked and gases can escape, so that although there is plenty of lava, few pyroclastic rocks are formed.

Ropy lava
As lava flows, the surface cools and forms a skin that wrinkles as the fluid center flows on.

Runny lavas
Basaltic lavas are fast-flowing and quickly spread to cover vast areas. This specimen of basalt was deposited by the Hualalai volcano on Hawaii.

Colorful crystals
Sparkling points in this basalt include green olivine and black pyroxene crystals.

Sedimentary rock

Weathered and eroded rocks break into smaller pieces of rock and minerals. This sediment may be transported to a new site (often a lake, river, or sea) and deposited in layers that become buried and compacted. Cemented together, the particles form new, sedimentary rocks.

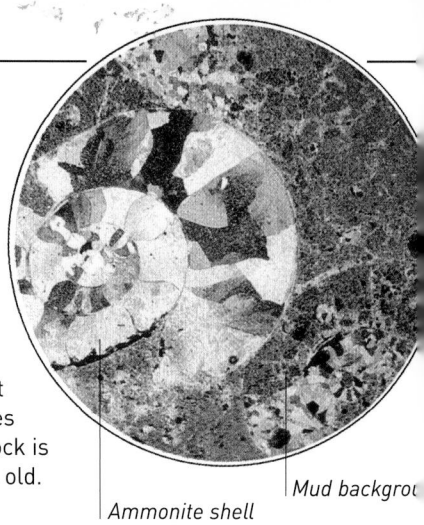

Thin section of limestone
Under the microscope, ammonite shells show up against the mud that buried them. Ammonites are now extinct—this rock is about 160 million years old.

Rock builders
Rarely bigger than a pinhead, foraminifera are marine organisms that secrete lime. When they die, the shells fall to the ocean floor, where they eventually become cemented into limestone.

Flint
A form of silica, lumps of flint are often found in limestones, especially chalk. They are gray or black, but may be covered in a white, powderlike material. Like obsidian, when flint is broken, it has a "conchoidal" fracture (see p. 48).

Limestone
Many sedimentary rocks consist of the remains of once-livi organisms. In these shelly and gastropod limestones, the remains animals are clearly visible in the rock. Chalk is a a limestone, formed from the skeletons of tiny s animals too small to see with t naked eye. Oolite, anoth limestone, forms in t sea as calcite builds around grains of sar As they are rolled and fro by waves, t grains become larg

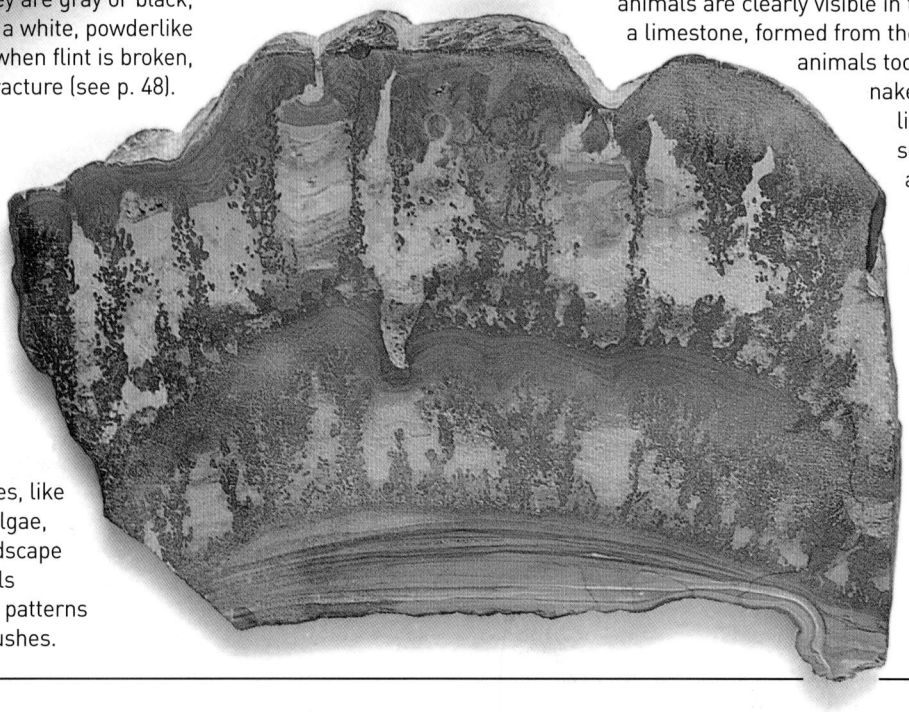

Algal limestone
So-called "muddy" limestones, like this one bound together by algae, are often referred to as "landscape marbles"—when the minerals crystallize they may produce patterns in the shapes of trees and bushes.

lcareous tufa
extraordinary looking evaporite, s porous rock is formed by the aporation of spring water and is metimes found in limestone caves.

Evaporites

Some sedimentary rocks are formed when saline waters (often seawater) evaporate and leave deposits of minerals. Examples include halite and gypsum. Halite is better known as rock salt, from which we get table salt. Gypsum is used to make plaster of Paris, and in its massive form it is called alabaster.

and Canyon, US
is site is eroded red ndstone and nestone.

Sandstones

Both these rocks are made from grains of sand cemented together. The red sandstone comes from a desert where wind rubbed and rounded the quartz grains. Grit is rougher—its more angular grains were buried before they could be rubbed smooth.

Clay

Formed of microscopically fine grains, clay feels sticky when wet. When it is compacted and all the water forced out of it, it forms hard rocks called mudstone or shale.

edded volcanic ash
many sedimentary rocks, individual ers of sediments form visible bands. re, the stripes are layers of volcanic h. The surface has been polished to hlight this feature.

Conglomerate

The flint pebbles in this rock were rounded by water as they rolled around on river- or seabeds. After they were buried, they became cemented together to form a rock known as conglomerate.

Breccia

Like conglomerate, breccias contain fragments of rock; however, these are much more angular as they have not been rounded by water or carried far from their original home—often at the bottom of cliffs.

Limestone

Limestone caves, lined with dripping stalactites and giant stalagmites, are formed when slightly acidic rainwater turns the limestone's carbonate into bicarbonate, which is soluble in water and is carried away.

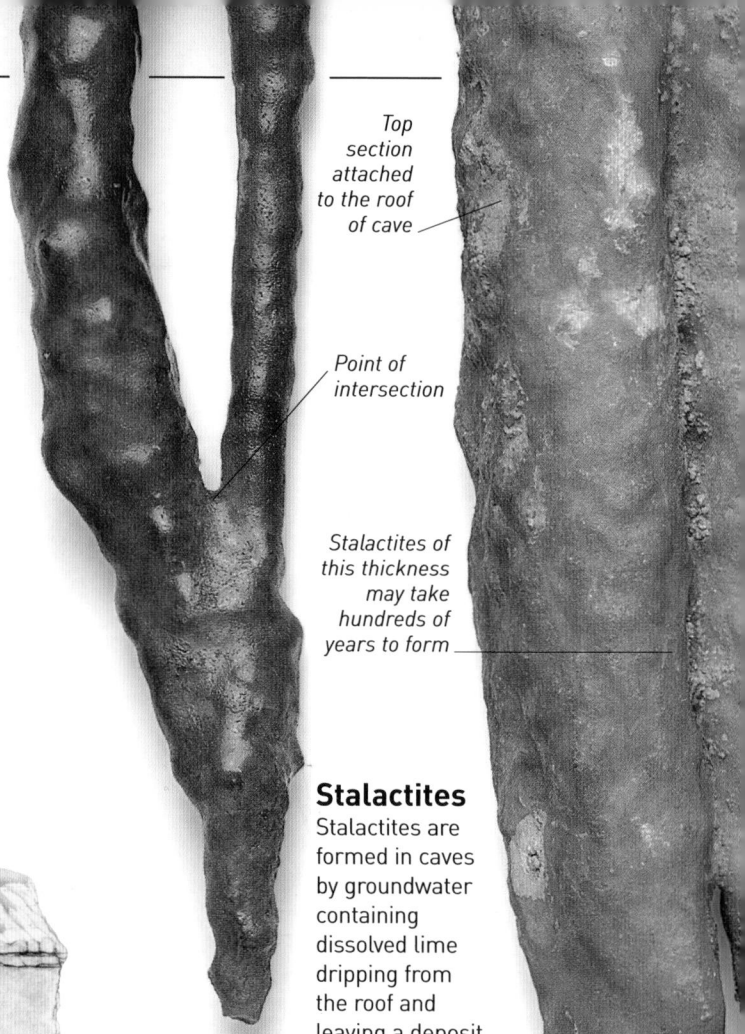

Single stalactite formed from two smaller ones growing together

Stalactites

Stalactites are formed in caves by groundwater containing dissolved lime dripping from the roof and leaving a deposit as it evaporates. Growing downward a a fraction of an inch each year—shown in annual growth rings—they may slowly reach many feet in length.

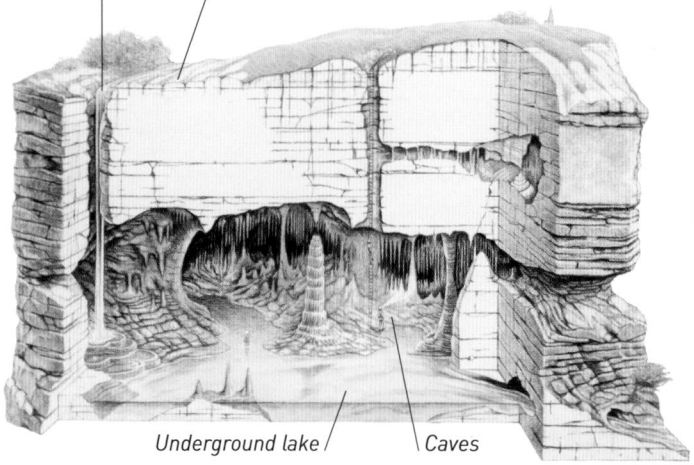

Limestone landscapes

Rainwater dissolves calcite in limestone, producing deep, narrow cracks ("grikes"). In time, the water enlarges them into passages. Flowing water dissolves the rock, producing "swallow holes" at the junctions between grikes. Underground streams form lakes in the caves.

Plan de Sales, France

Limestone pavements of flat blocks occur where weathering leaves no insoluble residue to make soil.

Tufa

A type of rock known as a precipitate, tufa forms when lime is deposited from water onto a rock surface in areas of low rainfall.

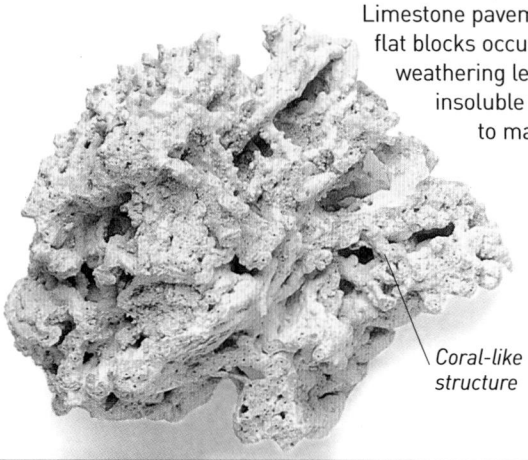

Ease Gill Caves, England

The forest of fine stalactites and stalagmites in this cave form the most spectacular part of a much larger, complex cave system under the hills of the Lancashire Pennines. In fact, this is the largest cave system in the UK.

Odd-shaped stalactite

Prominent growth rings mark the gradual development of the stalactite as successive deposits formed

Stone Forest, China

The staggering landscape of the Hunan Province of China is typical of "karst" scenery. Named after the limestone area of Karst in Yugoslavia, the term is applied to many limestone regions, including the Cumberland Plateau, Tennessee, parts of the Blue Mountains, Australia, and the Causses, France.

Point onto which overhead drips fall

range twin talactite

Last section to grow

Pamukkale Falls, Turkey

Beautiful travertine terraces are formed from the precipitation of calcite from hot springs in limestone areas. Travertine is quarried as a decorative building stone.

Stalagmites

Stalagmites are formed on the floor of caves where water has dripped from the roof or a stalactite above. As with stalactites, they develop as water containing dissolved lime evaporates.

If stalactites and stalagmites grow together and join, forming pillars, they are often described as "organ pipes," "hanging curtains," and "portcullises."

End attached to floor of the cave

Inside a stalactite

This specimen has been sliced through the center to reveal colored bands. The different colors show how the stalactite formed from deposits of lime with varying degrees of purity. The purest parts are the whitest.

Schist

Metamorphism

Metamorphic rocks are igneous or sedimentary rocks altered by heat and/or pressure. Such conditions can occur during the mountain-building process, as buried rocks are subjected to high temperatures and squeezed or folded, creating new minerals.

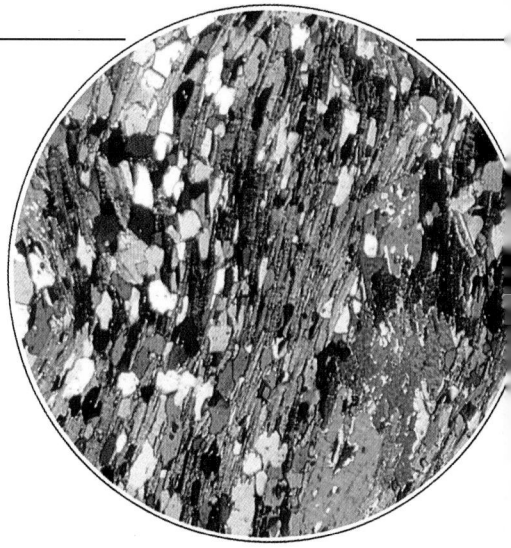

Thin section of garnet-mica schist
Seen through a petrological microscope, this rock reveals bright, blade-shaped mica crystals. Quartz and feldspar appear as shades of gray.

Saccharoidal marble

Evenly sized grains give a sugary appearance

Marbles

When limestone is exposed to very high temperatures, new crystals of calcite grow and form the compact rock known as marble. This can look similar to the rock, quartzite, but marble is softer and easily scratched with a knife. Some medium-grained marble looks sugary or "saccharoidal." The marble far right was made from limestone containing impurites, such as pyroxene.

Nodular gray marble

Pyroxene-bearing marble

Aggregates of carbon

Spotted slate

Chiastolite slate

Elongated chiastolite crystals

Spotted hornfels

From slate to hornfels

The irregular speckles in spotted slate are small aggregates of carbon, formed by heat from an igneous intrusion. In rocks nearer the intrusion, the temperature is considerably higher and needlelike crystals of chiastolite form in the slate. The rocks very close to the intrusion become so hot that they completely recrystallize and form a tough, new rock called hornfels.

Garnet-muscovite-chlorite schist

Kyanite-staurolite schist

19th-century slate quarry

Schists

Schist is formed from shale or mud but at a higher temperature than slate. The garnet-muscovite-chlorite schist was exposed to temperatures of at least 932°F (500°C). Kyanite-staurolite schist forms under high pressure, 6–9 miles (10–15 km) below ground.

late

uring mountain building, ale was squeezed so hard at its flaky micas crystallized right angles to the pressure. e resulting rock—slate—lits easily into thin sheets.

Biotite-kyanite gneiss

Banded gneiss

Gneisses

At high temperatures and pressures, sedimentary or igneous rocks may be metamorphosed to gneisses. These rocks have coarser grains than medium-grained schists and are easily identified because the minerals often separate into bands. These layers may be irregular where the rock has been folded under pressure.

clogite

roduced under very high pressure, eclogite is xtremely dense and is thought to form in the antle—far deeper than most other rocks. It ontains pyroxene and small, red crystals of garnet.

Migmatite

Under intense heat, parts of rocks may start to melt and flow, creating swirling patterns. This is very often shown in migmatites. They are not composed of one rock but are a mixture of a dark host rock with lighter-colored granitic rock. This sample is from the Scottish Highlands.

Marble

Marble is a metamorphosed limestone, but its name is often used in the stone industry for a variety of other rocks. All are valued for their attractive range of textures and colors, and because they are easily cut and polished.

In the raw
A true marble, this unpolished, coarsely crystalline specimen of Mijas Marble is from Malaga, Spain. Polishing will give it a smooth surface.

Medici Madonna
Michelangelo sculpted this statue from Carrara marble, c. 1530.

Greek connection
Originally from the Greek Island of Euboea, streaked Cipollino marble (above) is now quarried in Switzerland, the island of Elba, and Vermont.

Carrara quarry
The world's most famous marble comes from the Carrara quarry in Tuscany, Italy. It was the local stone for Michelangelo.

Italian specialty
Gray Bardilla marble (left) comes from the Carrara quarry.

Italian elegance
Another striking Italian marble (right) is the black-and-gold variety from Liguria.

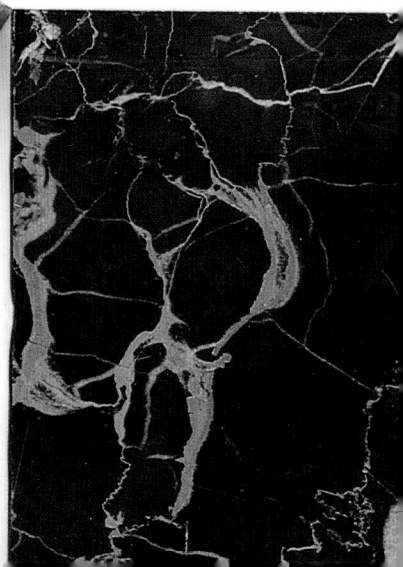

uscan tones
he distinctive exture of the Italian ecorative stone, Breccia ioletto, was the reason for its se in the Paris Opera House in 1875.

South African swirls
Polished travertine has beautiful swirling patterns. This piece is from Cape Province, South Africa.

aj Mahal, India
his monument uses many marbles.

Swiss origins
The limestone breccia known as Macchia-vecchia is quarried in Mendrisio, Switzerland.

Detail of marble inlay on the Taj Mahal

African copper
Quarried in Swaziland, Green Verdite's vivid coloring is caused by the presence of copper.

Algerian rock
Breche Sanguine or Red African (bottom) is a red breccia from Algeria. The Romans used it in the Pantheon, Rome, in the 1st century CE.

The first flint tools

Because flint splits in any direction, fractures to a sharp edge, and is fairly widespread, it was used in prehistoric times to make early tools and weapons.

Rough flint nodule found in chalk areas

Leather thong securing flint and antler sleeve to handle

Tools from flint

Flint was shaped by detaching flakes from a nodule to leave a core that gradually became more refined.

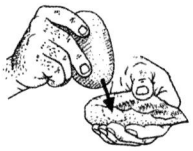

Stone-on-stone

Striking the flint with a stone created sharp, jagged edges.

Pressure-flaking

Pointed implements such as antler bones gave tools sharper cutting edges.

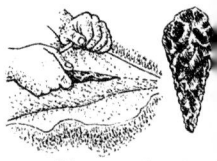

Sharp-edged to used for skinni

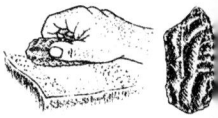

Scrapers we used to dre animal hid

Flint flakes and chippings

Cutting edge

Large, sharpened hand ax

Light-colored hand ax

Small, sharpened hand ax

Ear men usin hand axe

Crude early chopper

Rough cutting edge

Sharp cutting edge

Hand axes

Paleolithic hand axes were used to smash animal bones, skin hunted animals, and cut wood and plants. The well developed, dark axes are 70,000–300,000 years old. The lighter-colored ax dates from around 70,000–35,000 BCE.

solithic
ze
Antler sleeve
Hafted adzes were used to hollow out canoes
Danish ax and dagger
The shape of this Early Bronze Age ax, found in the Thames River in the UK, shows it was imported. Polished with care, it was clearly an object of value. So, too, was the Early Bronze Age flint dagger (2,300–1,200 BCE), which imitates the shape of the earliest copper daggers.
Ax
Flint dagger
Hafted adzes
Adzes have an asymmetrical cutting edge, with the blade at right angles to the handle. They were swung vertically to shape wood. These adzes date from the Mesolithic period (10,000–4,000 BCE).
Adze mounted directly onto handle
Asymmetrical cutting edge of flint
Arrowheads
The bow and arrow was invented in the Mesolithic period, and was still used for hunting in the Early Neolithic period, when leaf-shaped arrowheads were common. Later, in the Beaker period (2,750–1,800 BCE), barbed arrowheads were characteristic.
Neolithic arrow-heads
Beaker arrowheads
Sickle
Flint sickles show crops were cultivated. The long, slightly curved blade was swung sideways to reap crops. A "gloss" on their cutting edge shows repeated harvesting. This one is Neolithic (4,000–2,300 BCE).
Reproduction wooden handle
Flint daggers
Rare and made with care, these two daggers from the Beaker period were not just weapons, but status symbols, too.
Ninth-century obsidian ax from Mexico
Reproduction wooden handle
Spearhead with obsidian blade from the Admiralty Islands, off Papua New Guinea
Obsidian
Like flint, obsidian was used in early tools because it fractures with sharp edges.

Rocks as tools

Archeologists have found numerous examples of other stone implements besides flint, from many different cultures around the world. Some were used as weapons or status symbols, others as agricultural or domestic tools.

Brazilian stone ax

Neolithic ax showing a highly polished surface

Neolithic ax made of diorite, an igneous rock

Neolithic ax made of rhyolitic tuff, a volcanic rock

Stone axes

These stone axes date back to Neolithic Britain (4,000–2,300 BCE). Highly polished and tougher than flaked flint axes, they were traded over long distances—the source rocks were far from the places where the axes were found.

Wedge to stop the stone from moving

Bored quartzite pebble

Digging stic

During the Mesolithic a Neolithic periods (10,00 2,300 BCE), sticks weighted wi pierced pebbles were used break up the ground to pla crops or dig up roo

Breaking up ground with a digging stick prior to planting

Battle axes

These perforated axes belong to the Early Bronze Age (2,300–1,200 BCE) and are so well preserved that they could have been status symbols for display as well as for use as weapons. The bottom one was both an ax and a hammer.

Side view of battle ax made of diorit

Top view of battle ax

Reproduction wooden stick

Sharpened wooden point for digging hard ground

Carved stone maul (a war club or mace) made by Haida Indians, a North American tribe that lives on islands off British Columbia

South African digging stick with horn point and stone weight

Dual-purpose granite ax-hammer

Hammer end

Ax end

Engraved Viking forge stone made of soapstone and used in metalworking

Marble makeup palette

The Romans used powdered lead and chalk to whiten skin; red ocher to tint lips and cheeks; and soot to darken eyebrows. These were put on stone palettes, mixed with water or gum, and applied as a paint or paste.

Stone spindle whorl

To spin wool or cotton into thread, the Romans weighted a bone or wooden spindle with a stone whorl. The weight and rotating motion help twist the thread, which was then wound on to the spindle.

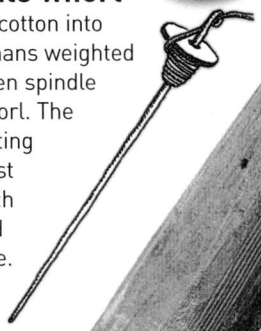

A bird-shaped mortar carved by Haida Indians

'hetstones

onze implements ere sharpened by bbing the blunt edge ainst a whetstone. ese two are Bronze e (2,300–700 BCE) and ere worn on a cord.

oman rotary quern

portable quern was used for grinding rn between two stones. The upper e was held in place by a spindle d was rotated by a handle. Grain s fed through the hole in the per stone, and the rotary otion forced it between e two grinding surfaces.

sing a quern to grind rn during the Iron Age

rain ady r grinding

Pigments

For body and rock art, early man crushed local rocks and mixed the powders with animal fats to produce a range of pigments. Over the centuries, as trading routes expanded, new colors were added to the artist's palette.

Earthy hue
Clays were widely us by early artists becau they were easy to sour and, being fine-grain easily pulverize

Color variation in a mineral
Many minerals are uniformly colored, but some come in a range of colors. For example, tourmaline (above) may occur as black, brown, pink, green, and blue crystals, or show a variety of colors in a single crystal.

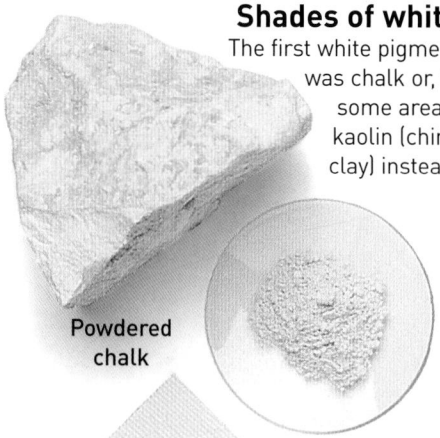

Shades of white
The first white pigment was chalk or, in some areas, kaolin (china clay) instead.

Cave paintin
The earliest known artworks wer made with a mixture of clays, chalk earths, and burned wood and bones

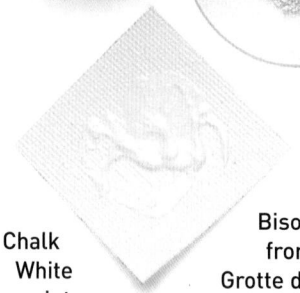

Bison from Grotte de Niaux, France, c. 20,000 BCE

Color clues
A useful aid when identifying a mineral is the color that it produces when you crush it. Or simply scrape a sample across an unglazed white tile—many minerals leave a distinct, colored streak, which may or may not be the same color as the mineral; others have no discernible streak.

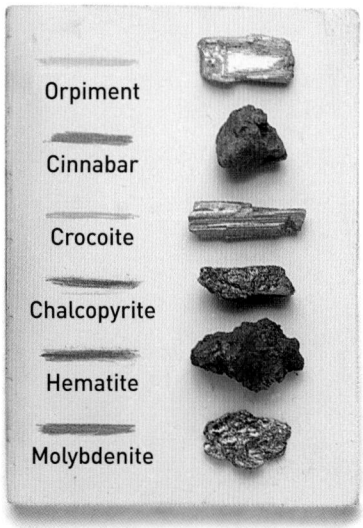

Black as coal
Still popular with artists today, charcoal was well-known to cave painters—from the embers of their fires.

in coloring
earthy variety of matite, an iron ore, duces a rich reddish-brown ment. Very finely powdered, it s also used as makeup for skin.

Egyptian orange
About 1,500 BCE, Egyptians first crushed realgar, an arsenic compound found in hot spring deposits, to form an orange pigment.

Bright gold
Medieval artists used orpiment, an arsenic compound, to make many colors and to imitate gold.

illiant green
nze-Age Egypt first used lachite, a copper compound, for green.

Precious blue
The refinement of lapis lazuli powder into a rich ultramarine (and expensive) blue was first achieved in Persia (now Iran).

Natural vermilion
The bright, vermilion red of cinnabar (mercuric sulfide) was used in prehistoric China, but only came into widespread use in the Middle Ages.

assical ue
e copper mpound urite produced ighly prized blue ment that was widely ed in classical antiquity.

Bright painting
By the late 13th century, artists were regularly using ultramarine and vermilion, as in this painting by Duccio.

Building stones

Most of the great monuments of the past survive because they were made from tough, natural stone. Today, natural building stones are mainly used for decoration, and man-mad materials for construction.

Quarrying in the early 19th century was still done almost entirely by manual labor

Nummulitic limestone
Formed 40 million years ago, nummulite, a foraminiferan, is a famous limestone from the same quarries that supplied stone for the pyramids near Cairo, Egypt.

The pyramids, Egypt, made of local limestone

Portland stone
After the Great Fire of London in 1666, St. Paul's Cathedral was rebuilt with this English limestone. The marks are made by "tooling," a decorative technique.

Oolitic limestone
This building stone formed some 160 million years ago.

Welsh slate

Christian mosaic
Small fragments of local stones were often used for mosaic floors.

Limestone used for roofing

Slate
Unlike most building materials, roofing stones must split easily into thin sheets. Slate is ideal, but where it was not available, builders used local, often inferior, stone.

Notre Dame, Paris
This famous cathedral in Paris, France, was built from local limestone from the St. Jacques region of the city, between 1163 and 1250. The catacombs in Paris are old quarries.

ranite
lished granite is often used the facades of buildings, in the imperial city of Petersburg, Russia.

Sandstones
Various colored sandstones make excellent building stones, as seen in many fine Mogul monuments in India.

Sandstone is 230 million years old

Red sandstone from Scotland used as a cladding building stone

Great Wall of China
At 1,500 miles (2,400 km) long, the world's biggest construction uses various materials that change with the terrain it passes through. Parts include brick, granite, and many local rocks.

Smooth red brick

Man-made

Even man-made stone substitutes, such as brick and tiles, cement, concrete, and glass, originate from rocks of some kind.

Early skyscraper
New York's Empire State Building was made of mostly granite and sandstone but also some man-made materials.

Roofing tiles
In many parts of the world, man-made roofing tiles are made from clay.

Textured buff brick

Bricks
Easily molded clays are fired to make bricks. Impurities in clays produce various colors and strengths.

Cement
Made by grinding and heating a limestone, cement mixed with sand, gravel, and water produces concrete.

The story of coal

The coal we burn is millions of years old. In the swampy forests of Asia, Europe, and North America, rotting leaves, seeds, and dead wood became buried. Overlying sediments squeezed out the water and compressed the plant matter into peat and then coal, layer upon layer. As pressure and heat grew, other types of coals were formed.

Fossilized wood
Jet is hard, black, but very light and is derived from driftwood laid down in the sea. Polished and carved, often for jewelry, it has been used since the Bronze Age.

Coal as jewelry
A major source of jet is Yorkshire, in northern England. These Roman pendants, found in York, were probably made of local jet.

Oil shale
A sedimentary rock, oil shale contains kerogen, an organic substance of plant and animal origin. When heated, kerogen gives off a vapor from which oil is extracted.

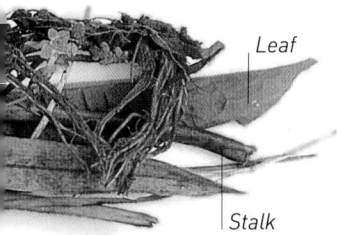

ed case

The origins of coal

Carboniferous swamps may have looked similar to this stylized engraving.

The raw ingredients of coal

In areas with thick layers of vegetation and poor drainage, such as swamps or bogs, dead plants become waterlogged. They start to rot, but cannot decay completely.

The peat layer

Peat is a more compact form of the surface layer of rotting plants. Some roots and seed cases are still visible. Newly formed peat can be cut, dried, and burned as a fuel.

Cutting peat

This Irish turf-cutter is cutting peat by hand; machines can also be used.

Brown coal

Naturally compressed peat forms crumbly, brown lignite that still contains recognizable plant remains. Undried peat is 90 percent water; lignite is 50 percent.

Coal seams

Layers of coal are called seams. They are sandwiched between layers of other material, such as sandstones and mudstones.

"Black gold"

Under pressure, lignite is converted into bituminous or household coal. Hard and brittle, it has a very high carbon content. A charcoal-like powdery substance makes the coal dirty to handle.

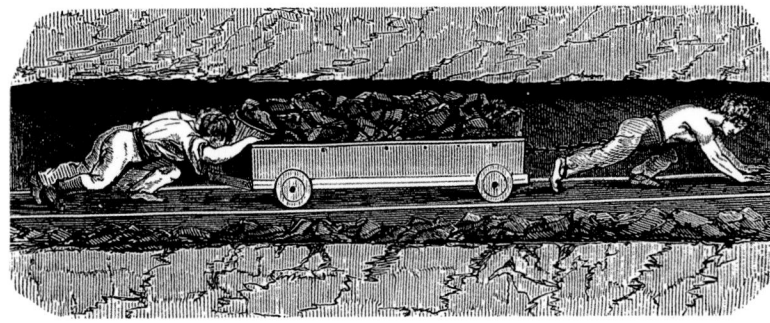

Children in a mine, 1842

During the Industrial Revolution, miners and their children worked long hours underground in terrible conditions.

Mining for coal

Coal has been mined since the Middle Ages. Some mines are open-cast, at the surface, but most are hundreds of feet beneath the land or sea.

The hardest coal

The highest-quality coal is anthracite. Shiny, harder than other coals, and clean to touch, it contains more carbon than the others, and it gives out the most heat and little smoke.

Fossils

Fossils are the evidence of past life preserved in the rocks of the Earth's crust. When an animal or plant is buried in sediment, usually the soft parts rot away, but the hardest parts remain—most fossils consist of the bones or shells of animals, or the leaves or woody parts of plants. In some marine fossils, shells may be replaced by other minerals, or an impression of the insides or outsides may be preserved. Fossils are found in sedimentary rocks, especially limestones and shales.

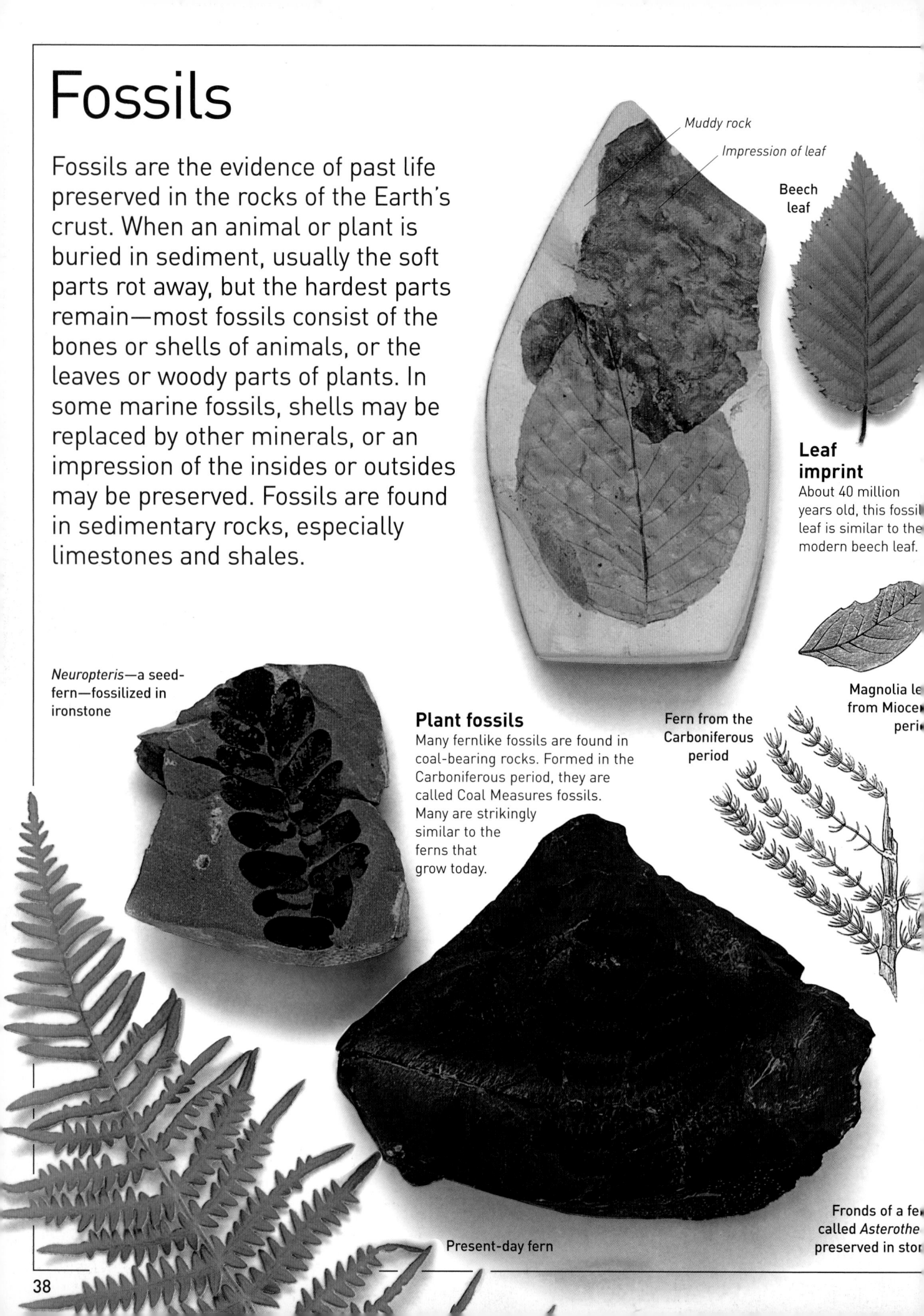

autilus

e nautilus shell is
vided into chambers. By
gulating the gas in these chambers,
e animal moves up or down in the water.

Ancient ancestors

This limestone (right) is about 200 million years old. It contains the remains of hundreds of ammonites. These sea creatures had hard, coiled shells, and are now extinct. Because ammonites changed rapidly and lived in many areas of the world, they can be used to determine the relative ages of the rocks in which they occur. The nearest modern equivalent to the ammonite is the nautilus.

A graveyard for snails

This piece of limestone (left) contains the hard spiral shells of marine gastropods (snails) from about 120 million years ago.

Fossil hunting

The abundance of fossils on seashores made collecting a popular pastime in the 19th century.

Space rocks

Every year about 19,000 meteorites each weighing over 4 oz (100 g) fall to Earth; most land in the sea or on deserts. Only about five are recovered annually. As they enter Earth's atmosphere, their surfaces melt and are swept away, but their cold interiors survive.

Pasamonte fireball
Photographed in New Mexico, this fireball fell to Earth in March 1933. Meteorites are named after the places where they fall—this one in Pasamonte. The fireball broke up in the atmosphere, heralding the fall of dozens of meteoritic stones.

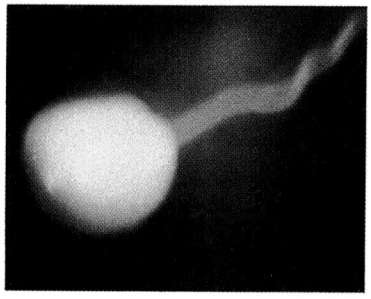

Fragme of meteori

Dark, glas fusion cru formed duri passage throu Earth's atmosphe

Gray interior consisting mainly of the minerals olivine and pyroxene

Metallic meteorite
The Cañon Diablo meteorite landed about 20,000 years ago. Iron meteorites like this one are rarer than stony meteorites and consist of an iron-nickel alloy. They once formed parts of small asteroids that broke up when they collided with Earth. The largest meteorite known is the iron Hoba, from Namibia, which weighs about 66 tons (60 metric tons).

Earth's contemporar
The meteorite above fell at Barwe Leicestershire, UK, on Christmas Ev 1965. It formed 4.6 billion years ag at the same time as Earth but another part of the solar system. every 10 meteorites seen to fa eight are "stones" like Barwe

Explosion crater
When the 16,500-ton (15,000-metric ton) Cañon Diablo meteorite hit Arizona, it exploded. It created a huge hole, the Meteor Crater, about ¾ mile (1.2 km) across and nearly 600 ft (180 m) deep. Only 33 tons (30 metric tons) of meteorite remained, scattered as small fragments across the surrounding countryside.

Metal and ston
Stony-irons form a separate grou of meteorites. This slice of the Thi Mountains meteorite shows brig metal enclosing stony material. was found in Antarctica, whe meteorites have la for about 300,0 years, large encase in ic

Metal

Stony part containing olivine

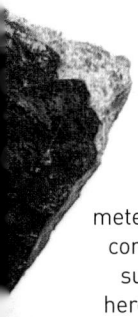

Halley's Comet
Water-bearing meteorites may have come from comets, such as Halley's—here depicted in the Bayeux tapestry.

Water-bearers
The Murchison meteorite fell in Australia in 1969. It contains carbon compounds and water, similar to the nucleus of a comet. Such meteorites are rare.

Asteroid structure
Many meteorites come from the collision of asteroids that circle the Sun, mostly between the orbits of Mars and Jupiter. They have a metal core, the source of some iron meteorites like Cañon Diablo; a core-mantle, the source of stony-iron meteorites like Thiel Mountains; a mantle, from which few meteorites are known; and an outer crust, the source of stony meteorites like Barwell.

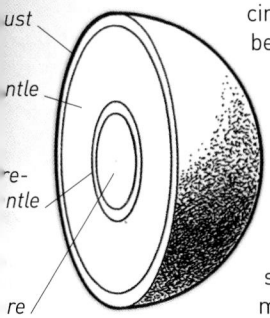

Rocks from the Moon and Mars

ve meteorites found in Antarctica are known to have come om the Moon because they are like lunar highlands rocks ollected by the Apollo missions. Eight other meteorites are ought to have come from Mars.

Martian origin
The Nakhla stone fell in Egypt in 1911. Only 1.3 billion years old, far younger than most meteorites, it probably came from Mars.

Lunar discoveries
he lunar meteorites are made of the same material as this boulder next to Apollo 17 astronaut, Jack Schmitt.

Moon rock
The Moon's surface is covered with soil made of rock and mineral fragments, from bombardment by meteorites. Similar material on the surface of an asteroid was compacted to form stony meteorites. Here, the white minerals are feldspar, the darker ones pyroxene.

Minerals

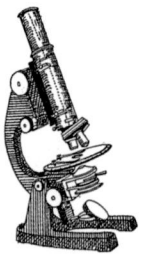

Petrological microscope

Eight elements make up nearly 99 percent of Earth's crust, combining to form minerals that form rocks. Certain mineral groups are typical of certain rocks. Silica minerals predominate in common, mostly igneous, rocks.

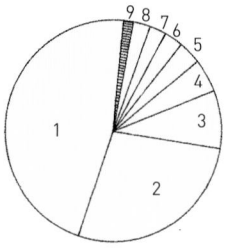

Crust's makeup
In weight order: oxyge (1), silicon (2), aluminu (3), iron (4), calcium (5 sodium (6), potassium magnesium (8), and al other elements (9).

Minerals in granitic rocks

Feldspars, the most common minerals, plus quartz, micas, and amphiboles form granitic and dioritic rocks.

Group of black prismatic crystals with calcite

Single hornblende crystal

Hornblende, an amphibole, common in igneous and some metamorphic rocks

Tremolite, common in metamorphic rocks

Silvery, radiating, needlelike crystals

Amphiboles
This group of minerals is widely found in igneous and metamorphic rocks. They can be distinguished from pyroxenes (opposite) by the characteristic angles between their cleavage planes (p.48).

Quartz or rock crystal

Silica minerals
These include quartz, chalcedony, and opal. Quartz is one of the most widely distributed minerals, occuring in igneous, sedimentary, and metamorphic rocks.

Potassic feldspar
Orthoclase is found many metamorphic a igneous rocks. lower-temperatu form is microclin

Green microcline (or amazonstone) crystal

Twinned crystals of white orthoclase

Thin section of a diorite
Viewed under the special light of a petrological microscope, this diorite reveals colored amphiboles, plain gray to white quartz, and is lined gray plagioclase feldspar.

Biotite, a dar iron-rich mica usual found in igneous rock

Muscovite, an aluminum-rich mica

Silvery brown tabular crystals

Micas
There are two main types of mica: dark iron- and magnesium-rich mica, and white aluminum-rich mica. All have perfect cleavage, splitting into thin flakes.

asic rocks

e minerals shown here
e all found in basic rocks
e basalts and gabbros.

Pink crystals of anorthite, a
agioclase feldspar, with augite

inned crystals
albite with
cite

Nepheline, a
feldspathoid,
with calcite

agioclase
ldspars

mmon in
neous rocks,
ese minerals
bove) contain
dium and calcium.

eldspathoids

ese minerals have less silica than
dspars and typically form in volcanic lavas.

Olivine

This silicate of iron and magnesium is typically found in silica-poor rocks, such as basalts, gabbros, and peridotites. It often forms as small grains or large, granular masses.

Green olivine crystals

Crystals of olivine,
from Vesuvius

Single crystal
of augite

Thin section of a basalt

Olivine basalt reveals brightly colored olivine, brown-yellow pyroxene, and minute gray plagioclase feldspars.

Volcanic rock

Crystal of leucite,
a feldspathoid

Prismatic crystal of
enstatite with biotite

Greenish-black
prismatic crystals of
augite, a pyroxene

Pyroxenes

The most common pyroxenes are calcium, magnesium, and iron silicates. Augite is a widely distributed pyroxene. Enstatite is less common.

)ther groups

arbonates and clays are two
ore groups of rock-
rming minerals.

arbonates

ese are key
nstituents
sedimentary
mestones) or
etamorphic
arble) rocks.
e most
mmon is
lcite, in
nestones.

lomite, a carbonate, found in some sedimentary
posits usually interbedded with limestones

Montmorillonite

Illite

Kaolinite (china clay) formed from
partly decomposed orthoclase

Clays

Part of the sedimentary rock sequence, clays form from the weathering and alteration of aluminous silicates.

Crystals

Snowflake

The word crystal comes from the Greek word *kryos*, meaning icy cold—rock crystal, a form of quartz, was once thought to be deep-frozen ice. In fact, a crystal is a solid, with a regular internal structure. Due to the arrangement of its atoms, it may form smooth external surfaces called faces. Many crystals have commercial uses, and some are cut as gemstones.

Crystal collecting in the Alps, c. 1870

Crystals orientated in random growth directions

Light reflecting on the crystal face

Parallel striations (lines) formed as the crystal grew

Large twinned crystal

Plane of intersection

Well developed faces

"Ice" sculpted by nature

This beautiful group of rock crystal found in Isère, France, is particular well formed, consisting of a large twin crystal and many simple crystals. The narrow ridges and furrows across some of its faces ar called striations. These were forme when two different crystal faces trie to develop at the same time.

rystal symmetry

ystals can be grouped into seven systems according their symmetry, which is shown in certain regular atures of the crystal. For example, for every face ere may be another on the opposite side of the ystal that is parallel to it and similar in shape and e. But in most mineral specimens it can be difficult determine the symmetry because crystals occur aggregates and do not have well developed faces.

What's the angle?

Since the angle between corresponding faces of a particular mineral is always the same, scientists measure the angle with a contact goniometer to help identify the mineral.

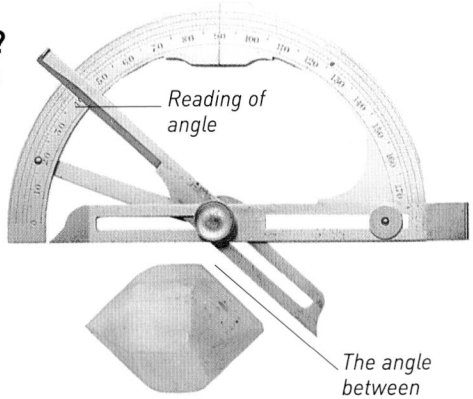

iclinic

is system's crystals display the least symmetry, shown by this wedge-shaped axinite crystal.

Cubic

Metallic pyrite forms cube-shaped crystals, but other cubic mineral forms include octahedra and tetrahedra. Crystals in this system exhibit the highest symmetry.

Tetragonal

Dark-green vesuvianite crystals are grouped with zircon and wulfenite in the tetragonal system.

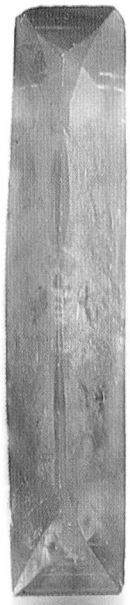

Orthorhombic

Common crystals in this sytem include olivine, topaz, and baryte (right), the source of barium for medical use.

onoclinic

e most common crystal system cludes gypsum (from which make plaster of Paris), urite, and orthoclase.

Rhombohedral (trigonal)

Smaller secondary crystals have grown on this siderite crystal. Quartz, tourmaline, corundum, and calcite belong to the same system.

Hexagonal

Beryl, including this emerald variety, crystallizes in the hexagonal system, as do apatite and ice and snowflakes.

Snowflakes

winning

cavities in mineral veins, ystals may grow in oups. Sometimes o (or possibly ore) individual ystals appear intersect in a mmetrical manner; ese are known as winned crystals."

Contact twins

The mineral cerussite crystallizes in the orthorhombic system, like this group of twin crystals (left).

Penetration twins

Staurolite is also an orthorhombic mineral. In this cross-shaped specimen, one twin appears to penetrate into the other.

Twinned gypsum crystals form an arrow-shape from which they get their common name, "swallow-tail"

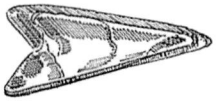

Crystal growth

No two crystals are exactly alike because the conditions in which they develop vary. They range from microscopic to several yards long. The shape of a crystal or aggregate of crystals constitute its "habit."

White coral
Aragonite, named after the Spanish province of Aragon, can sometimes ha a "coralloid" (coral-shaped) habit.

Radiating needles
Slender, elongated crystals are said to have an "acicular" (needlelike) habit. In this scolecite specimen, gray acicular crystals radiate from the center.

Metallic "grapes"
Some chalcopyrite crystals grow outward from a center and such aggregates appear as rounded nodules. The habit is "botryoidal" meaning "like a bunch of grapes

Sparkling aggregate
Hematite occurs in several habits. When it forms shiny, reflective crystals, it is said to have a "specular" habit, as in this aggregate.

Crystal columns
"Prismatic" crystals, such as this beryl crystal, are muc longer in one direction than in the other two.

Soft strands
These crystals of tremolite are very soft and pliable. Minerals with this habit are known as asbestos.

Thin sheets
Mica splits into sheets and is said to be "micaceous" or "foliated" (leaflike) or "lamellar" (thin and plated).

Equal side
Many minerals develop crystals th are essentially equal in all dimension these are said to be "equan This specimen of garnet in mi schist is a fine exampl

ual form

rite crystallizes as cubes and as 12-faced ids called pentagonal dodecahedra. If the nditions change during growth, both forms y codevelop, with striations on the faces.

Parallel lines

During crystal growth a series of crystals of the same type may develop in the same direction. This calcite aggregate shows a number of tapering pale pink and gray crystals in perfect parallel orientation.

Salt lake, Cyprus

When salt lakes dry up, a thick crust of soluble salts is left.

Hopper growth

The mineral halite (salt) is cubic, but crystals can grow from solution faster along the cube edge than in the center of the faces, resulting in the formation of "hopper crystals" that have stepped cavities in each face.

Stepped crystals

This halite contains numerous sand grains. It grew along preferred axes, forming a stack of cubic crystals in steps.

Double-decker

Chalcopyrite and halerite crystals have similar structures. ere, tarnished, brassy chalcopyrite crystals have grown in parallel on brownish-black sphalerite crystals.

ranching metal

a restricted space, as between two beds of ck, native copper and other minerals may ow in thin sheets. Its characteristic anchlike form is described "dendritic."

Phantom growth

The dark areas within this quartz crystal formed when a thin layer of chlorite coated the crystal at an earlier stage of its growth. As the crystal continued to grow, the chlorite became a ghostlike outline.

The properties of minerals

Most minerals have a regular crystal structure and a definite chemical composition. These determine the chemical and physical properties that are characteristic for each mineral and help geologists to identify it and see how it was formed.

Structure

Some chemically identical minerals exist in more than one form. For example, the element carbon forms two minerals: diamond and graphite.

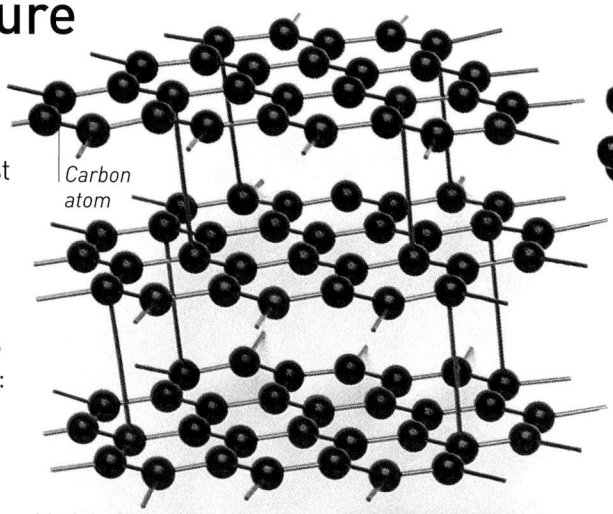

Model of graphite structure

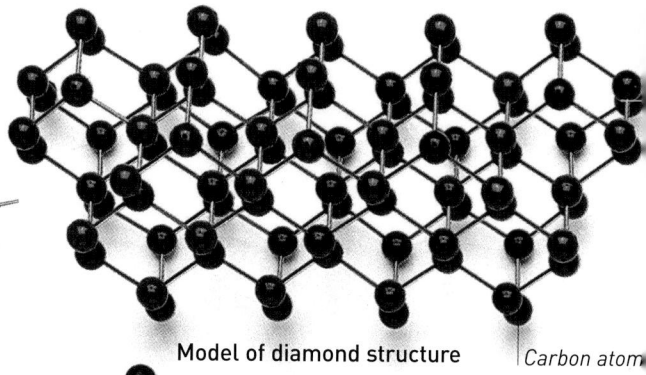

Model of diamond structure

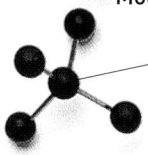

Model showing how one atom is bonded to four others

Graphite

In this hexagonal mineral formed under high temperatures, each carbon atom is closely linked to three others in the same plane. Built up of widely spaced layers only weakly bonded together, graphite is very soft (Mohs' scale 1–2).

Graphite specimen

Diamonds

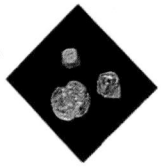

Diamond

In this cubic mineral formed under high pressure, each carbon atom is strongly bonded to four other to form a rigid and compact structure. Diamond is extremely hard (Mohs' scale 10).

Cleavage

When crystals break, some tend to split along well-defined cleavage planes, due to their atoms' orderly arrangement.

Thin sheets

Stibnite shows a sheetlike cleavage due to weakly bonded chains of antimony and sulfur atoms.

Lead steps

Galena, the main ore of lead, has a cubic cleavage, due to the arrangement of its lead and sulfur atoms. A split face has small cubic steps.

Perfect break

Baryte crystals show two perfect cleavages. If this crystal were broken, it would split along these planes.

Perfect rhomb

Calcite has such a well developed rhombohedral cleavage that a break in any other direction is virtually impossible.

Fracture

Quartz crystals break with a glassy, conchoidal (shell-like) fracture, not along a particular plane.

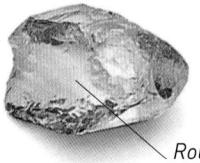

lardness

e bonds holding atoms together dictate a mineral's hardness. 1812, mineralogist Friedrich Mohs devised a scale of hardness at is still in use today. He chose 10 minerals as standards and nked them so that any mineral on the scale would scratch ly those below it.

Relative hardness
The intervals between the minerals in Mohs' scale are irregular. Diamond is about 40 times harder than talc, while corundum is only nine times as hard.

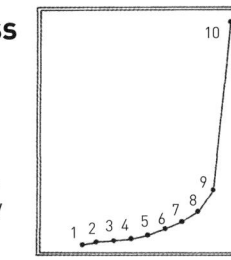

1	2	3	4	5	6	7	8	9	10
Talc	Gypsum	Calcite	Fluorite	Apatite	Orthoclase	Quartz	Topaz	Corundum	Diamond

Magnetism

nly two common inerals, magnetite d pyrrhotite (both on compounds), are rongly magnetic. agnetite lodestones ere used as an early rm of compass.

atural magnet
rmanently magnetized agnetite attracts iron ngs and other metallic ects such as paper clips.

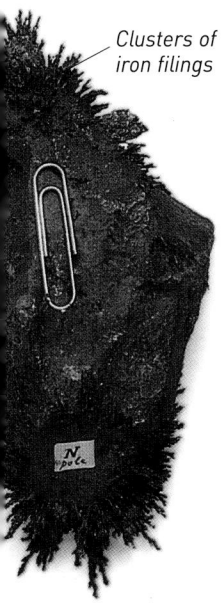

Optical

The optical effect as light passes through a mineral is due to light's interaction with atoms in the structure.

Double daisy
Light traveling through a calcite rhomb is split into two rays, which makes one stem look like two.

Fluorescing autunite
Viewed under ultraviolet light, certain minerals fluoresce.

Specific gravity

Specific gravity is defined as the ratio of the weight of a substance to that of an equal volume of water. Determining the specific gravity may aid identification.

Size vs. weight
The nature of the atoms and internal atomic arrangement of a mineral determines its specific gravity. These three mineral specimens are different sizes but weigh the same, as the atoms in quartz and galena are heavier or more closely packed together than the atoms in mica.

Gemstones

Gem-studded ornament

Gemstones are minerals of great beauty, rarity, and resilience. Light reflects and refracts with the minerals to produce the intense colors of gems, such as ruby and emerald, and the "fire" of diamond. Color, fire, and luster are revealed by skilled cutting and polishing for use in jewelry. Gems are usually weighed by the carat, equal to one-fifth of a gram.

Diamond

Diamond is named from the Greek word *adamas* ("unconquerable"). It is the hardest mineral of all and is famed for its lasting fiery brilliance. The quality of a gem diamond is measured by the four Cs: its color, clarity, cut, and carat weight.

Kimberley diamond mine, South Africa

Diamonds in rock

Kimberlite is the source rock for most diamonds. It is named after Kimberley in South Africa, where it occurs in a volcanic pipe that has its roots 100–200 miles (160–320 km) deep in Earth's crust.

Treasures in gravel

Until 1870 diamond crystals and fragments cam from river gravels, mostly in India or Brazil. The South Africa's diamond-ri kimberlite made it th leading supplier.

Multi-colored diamonds

Diamonds range from colorless through yellow and brown to pink, green, blue, and a very rare red. Table, rose, and brilliant cuts display their fire and luster to best advantage.

Beryl

Beautiful, hexagonal beryl crystals are found in many countries. Emerald and aquamarine, two major gem varieties, have long been exploited. Egyptian emerald mines date back to 1650 BCE.

Cut emerald

Emeralds

The best emeralds, like those in the British Crown Jewels, occur in veins with calcite and pyrite, in Colombia. Flawless emeralds are very rare and most crystals contain small blemishes or mineral inclusions.

Roman beryl

The earrings and necklaces contain cut emeralds.

Aquamarine

Yellow heliodor

Greenish heliodor

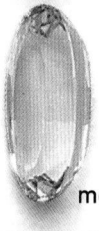

Pink morganite

Beryl's assorted colors

Pure beryl is colorless. The gems' colors are due to impurities, such as the manganese that makes morganite pink. Aquamarine can be made bluer with heat.

Crown jewel

The Koh-i-noor Indian diamond, worn here by Queen Mary, was given to Queen Victoria in 1850.

orundum

by and sapphire are varieties of the mineral rundum, which is colorless when pure. Tiny antities of chromium give e to the red of ruby. Iron d titanium give e blues, yellows, d greens of sapphire.

ar sapphire

nes with fine, needlelike stals orientated in three ections can be cut as star ies or star sapphires.

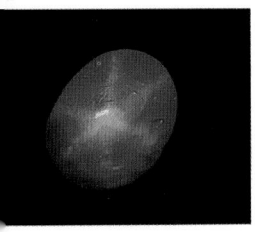

The Edwardes Ruby

This exceptional crystal weighs 162 carats. It is almost certainly from the famous gem deposits of Mogok, Myanmar (Burma).

Sapphire crystal

Ruby tends to form in flat crystals, while sapphire tends to be barrel-shaped or pyramidal, often with zones of blue to yellow color.

River jewels

Most sapphires and rubies come from gem-rich gravels. The gems are harder and less weathered than the parent rocks filtered out in riverbeds.

Gems in jewelry

The oldest jewelry comes from burials 20,000 years ago. Here, rubies, emeralds, and diamonds decorate a late-16th-century enameled, gold pendant.

Cut ruby

Gem sources

Australia supplies the most blue and yellow sapphires. Rubies are mined in Myanmar, Thailand, and central Africa. Sri Lanka is famous for blue and pink sapphires.

Blue sapphire

Colorless sapphire

Pink sapphire

Yellow sapphire

Clear sapphire

Mauve sapphire

pal

pal probably gets its name from India, om the Sanskrit word *upala* ("precious one"). Roman jewelry used pals from the Czech epublic. In the 1500s, pal came from Central merica. After 1870, ustralia became e leading upplier.

pal's rocky origins

ost opal forms over long periods of time in sedimentary cks, like this sample from Australia, but in Mexico and e Czech Republic it forms in gas cavities in volcanic rocks. pal is often cut as cabochons, but the veins in sedimentary cks are often thin. Slices may be glued onto onyx or glass to rm doublets, and capped with clear quartz to form a triplet.

Opal mining in Australia

In addition to its use in jewelry, opal mined today is also used in the manufacture of abrasives and insulation products.

Iridescent black opals

Color variations in opal

Opal's blue, green, yellow, and red iridescence is caused by light from minute silica spheres within the mineral. The "body" color can be clear, milky, white, or either gray or black in its most precious form.

White opal

Milky opal

Fire opal

The finest fire opal comes from Mexico and Turkey and is usually cut as faceted stones. It is valued as much for its intensity of color as for its iridescence.

Decorative stones

Turquoise, agate, lapis lazuli, and jade are all gems made up of many crystals. They are valued mainly for their color, evenly distributed as in turquoise, or patterned as in an agate cameo. Agate and jade are also tough, ideal for fine carving.

Chalcedony

Cornelian, onyx, chrysoprase, and agate are all forms of chalcedony. Pure chalcedony is translucent gray or white and consists of thin layers of tiny quartz fibers. Impurities create the patterns in agate.

Chrysopr
caboc

Ancient favorite
Apple-green chrysoprase has bee
used in jewelry since pre-Roman
times, often in cameos or intaglio

Lapis lazuli

This blue gem consists mainly of lazurite and sodalite minerals with white calcite and specks of brassy-colored pyrite.

Purest samples
The best lapis lazuli is mined in Badakhshan, Afghanistan, where it occurs in lenses and veins in white marble.

Turquoise

Found in the earliest jewelry, turquoise gives its name to "turquoise-blue," a pale greenish-blue. Its color is largely due to copper and traces of iron. The more iron present, the greener the stone.

Cut turquoise
The finest sky-blue turquoise has been mined in Nishapur, Iran, for 3,000 years. Another ancient source, known to the Aztecs, is in the US Southwest, which now supplies most of the world's turquoise.

Lapis jewelry
Long used for beads and carvings, lapis has been known for more than 6,000 years and is named from the Persian word *Lazhward* ("blue").

Mesopotamian mosaic
Lapis was used to decorate the wooden box known as the Standard of Ur (detail above), c. 2,500 BCE.

Turquoise ornaments
This artifact may be of Persian origin. The double-headed serpent (top) is from an Aztec necklace.

True blue
The vivid blue of this lapis slice (left) is caused by small amounts of sulfur.

Egyptian amule
Many fine carvings hav
been recovere
from the tomb
of Egyptia
pharaoh

Agate
Banded agates form in cavities in volcanic rocks. Uruguay and Brazil are prolific sources.

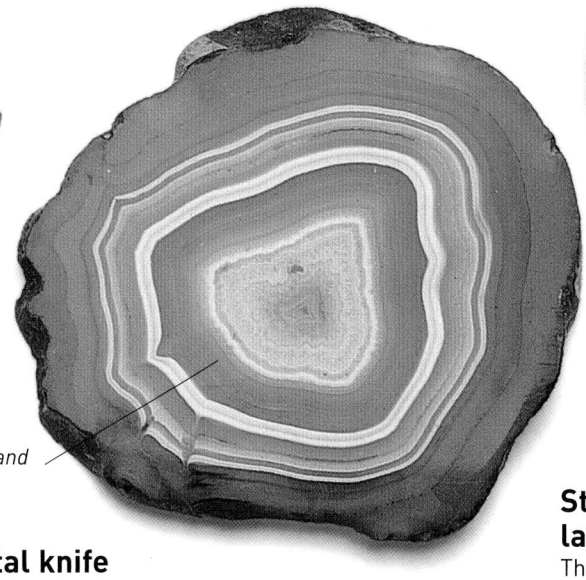

Polished sliced agate
Microscopic crystals formed in bands as hot, silica-rich solutions filtered through cavities in porous rocks.

Cameo portrait
This bloodstone shows a Roman emperor.

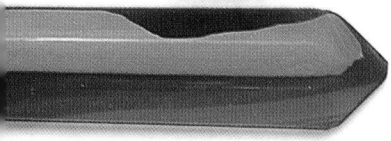

Ornamental knife
Cornelian is red chalcedony and has been used in jewelry and inlay work throughout history.

Stone landscape
The pattern in moss agate or mocha stone is shown to advantage in this delicate cabochon.

Jade

Named from the Spanish *piedra de hijada* used to describe the green stone carved by the Indians in Central America, jade refers to two different substances—jadeite and nephrite.

utankhamun's mask
pis, cornelian, obsidian, artz, and colored glass are aid in gold.

Rare jade
Jadeite can be white, orange, brown, lilac, or the translucent green "imperial jade."

Chinese art
The toughness of jade was known to the Chinese more than 2,000 years ago and this was exploited in their delicate carvings.

Mogul dagger
Mogul craftsmen carved pale green and gray nephrite into dagger handles, bowls, and jewelry, often inlaid with rubies and other gems.

Nephrite boulder
Nephrite is more common than jadeite and is generally green, gray, or creamy white. Much jade occurs as waterworn boulders, as in this example from New Zealand.

Other gems

Mughal emperor Shah Jahan

In addition to well-known gemstones such as diamond, ruby, sapphire, emerald, and opal, many other minerals have been used for human adornment. These are just some of the stones frequently seen in jewelry, but the full range of luster, fire, and color is extensive.

Multicolored topaz

Blue topaz

Yell top

Topaz
Occuring chiefly in granites and pegmatites, some gem-quality topaz crystals are very large, weighing many pounds. The largest stones are colorless or pale blue, but the most valuable are golden-yellow imperial topaz or pink topaz.

Blue spinel

Pink spinel

Mauve spinel

Spinel
Red spinels resemble rubies and were once called balas rubies, after Balascia, now Badakhshan in Afghanistan. There is also a range of pink, lilac, blue, and bluish-green stones.

Cut spinel

Black Prince's Ruby
This famous spinel is the central stone in the British Imperial State Crown.

Topaz brooch
Brown topaz was commonly used in 18th- and 19th-century jewelry. Yellow topaz was heated to turn it pink.

Perid
This is the transparent gem variety olivine. The proportion of iron in the miner determines the shade of color. The mo valuable golden-green and deep-gre stones contain less iron than those w a brownish tinge. Peridot h been used in jewelry sin classical times, a originally came from t island of Zebirget the Red Se

Vermilion zircon

Pink zircon

Green zircon

Yellow zircon

Blue zircon

Zircon
Named from *zargoon*, the Arabic word for vermilion or golden colored, stones of these colors as well as green and brown have long been used in Indian jewelry. Transparent stones are cut and polished for a luster and fire similar to diamond, but they are softer and chip more easily.

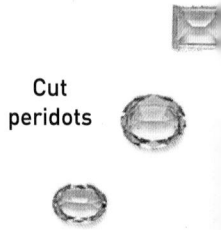

Cut peridots

arnet

rnet is a group name for a diverse set of gems that includes nandine and pyrope (red and purplish-red), spessartine ange-red), grossular (orange, green, or colorless), and mantoid (green). Fine demantoid rivals emerald for color and exceeds diamond for fire. Its beauty and rarity command a high price.

Garnet earrings

Rose-cut stones make attractive jewelry when set in gold, as shown by these 18th-century earrings.

Rose-cut stone

Gold

Grossular garnets

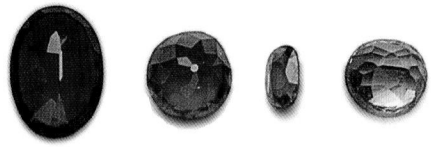

Almandine Hessonite Pyrope Demantoid

Demantoid garnets

reek diadem

is section of an Hellenistic diadem dates from the d century BCE and is inlaid with garnets. Its design common to many Greek artifacts of that time.

urmaline

urmaline shows the greatest range in color of any gemstone, and me single crystals are multicolored. The crystal forms and ctrical properties are different at each end of a crystal—this larity is sometimes reflected in color differences, especially pink d green. Cut stones can show this variation to advantage.

Amethyst

Purple amethyst is a variety of quartz. Colorless, transparent rock crystal is the purest form of quartz, and the colors of amethyst, citrine (yellow quartz), and rose quartz are caused by iron or titanium impurities.

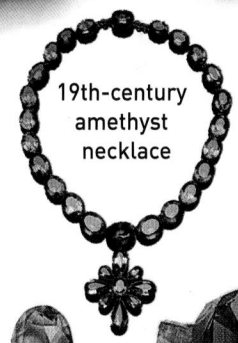

19th-century amethyst necklace

Cut amethyst

llowish-een urmaline

Green tourmaline

Blue tourmaline

Pink tourmaline

Brown tourmaline

Mauve-gray tourmaline

"Watermelon" tourmaline

Graduating color tourmaline

Byzantine relic, c. 955 CE

Many Byzantine artifacts were made of gold and decorated with precious stones.

Ore minerals

Mined, quarried, or dredged from lakes and rivers, ore minerals are crushed and separated, then refined and smelted (fused and melted) to produce metal. Copper was in use well before 5000 BCE. Around 3000 BCE, tin was added to make a harder metal, bronze. Iron was even harder and was widespread by 500 BCE.

Bronze ritual food vessel from China, c. 10th century BCE

Bauxite—aluminum ore

Lightweight aluminum

Aluminum is a good conductor of electricity, lightweight, not easily corroded, and used in power lines and saucepans.

Aluminum foil

Stacks of aluminum ingots

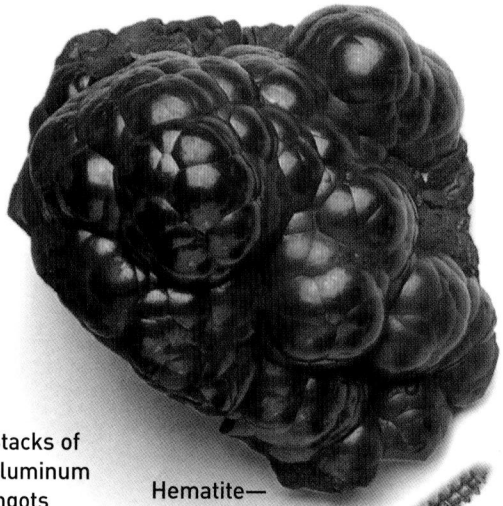

Hematite—iron ore

Steel screw

Iron mining, c. 15

Tough irc

Hematite is the most importa iron ore. Iron is tough and ha yet easy to work. It can be ca forged, machined, rolled, a alloyed with other meta Steel is made from irc

Rutile—titanium ore

Colorful copper

Brassy, yellow chalcopyrite and bluish-purple bornite are common copper ores. Because it is a good conductor, copper is used in the electricity industry, and because it is malleable (easy to shape and roll), it is good for household water pipes. It is also used in alloys with zinc (brass) and with tin (bronze).

Strong titanium

Rutile and ilmenite are the main ores of titanium. Usually found in igneous or metamorphic rocks, these two minerals form deposits with other minerals, many of which are extracted as by-products. Lightweight yet very strong, titanium is widely used in aircraft frames and engines.

Airliner partially constructed from titanium

Copper plumbing joint

ivanized
l

ack jack zinc

nalerite or "black
k," as it was
own by miners, is
most important
c ore and is found
deposits in volcanic
d sedimentary
cks. Zinc is used
galvanizing—
ating sheet steel
h a thin layer of
c to prevent it
m rusting.

Durable nickel

Nickel comes from deposits in large, layered gabbroic intrusions and from deposits formed by the weathering of basaltic igneous rocks. Nickeline occurs in small amounts in silver and uranium deposits where nickel is a by-product. Nickel is used in corrosion-resistant alloys, such as stainless steel and in high-temperature, high-strength alloys suitable for aircraft and jet engines.

Red mercury

The poisonous mercury ore cinnabar forms close to recent volcanic rocks and hot springs. Mercury is very dense, has a low melting point, and is liquid at room temperature. It is widely used in drugs, pigments, insecticides, and scientific instruments.

oft and shiny lead

lena, the main lead ore, is
rked chiefly from deposits in
nestones. Lead is the densest
d softest common metal, with
igh resistance to corrosion,
t it is not very strong.
s used in storage
tteries, gas,
gineering and
umbing, and
th tin in solder.

alena—
ad ore

Workable tin

The tin ore cassiterite is hard, heavy, and resistant to abrasion. Modern uses of tin are based on its resistance to corrosion, low melting point, malleability, lack of toxicity, and high conductivity. It is used in solder and tinplate. Pewter is an alloy with roughly 75 percent tin and 25 percent lead.

Precious metals

Gold and silver were among the first metals discovered. Valued for beauty and rarity, they—and platinum in the last 100 years—are used in coins to prove wealth, buy, and sell, and in jewelry and other objects.

Silver

Long used in coinage, but less valuable than gold or platinum, silver tarnishes easily. Sterling and plated silver are made into jewelry and ornaments.

Mexic ore-crush
Early method crushing silver o were primi but effect

Delicate silver wires
Silver is now mostly extracted as a by-product from copper and lead-zinc mining. Until the 20th century, it was mostly mined as native metal, like the famous silver "wires" from Norway.

Celtic brooch
The Celts fashioned ma intricate piece of jewelry in silver.

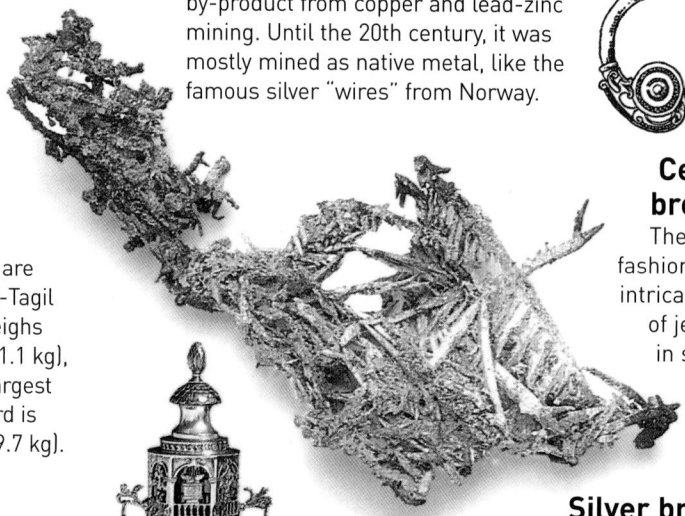

Silver branch
Occasionally, as in this specimen fr Copiapo, Chile, silver occurs in delica branchlike dendritic forn

Platinum

Now more valuable than gold, platinum is used in oil refining and in reducing pollution from car exhausts.

Sperrylite crystal
Platinum is found in several minerals, one being sperrylite. This is the largest known sperrylite crystal, found in South Africa c. 1924.

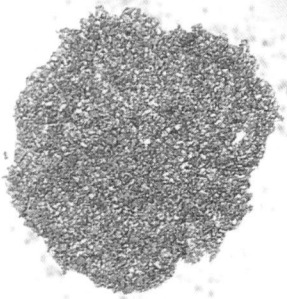

Platinum grains
Most platinum minerals occur as tiny grains in nickel deposits. These grains are from Colombia, where platinum was first reported in the 18th century.

Imperial coins
Platinum has been used as coinage in several countries, including Russia.

Platinum nugget
Large nuggets of platinum are rare. This one, from Nizhni-Tagil in the Urals, weighs 2 lb 6½ oz (1.1 kg), but the largest on record is 21 lb (9.7 kg).

Religious bell
One of a pair, this silver Torah bell was made in Italy in the early 18th century and was used in Jewish ceremonies.

Gold

Today, this metal is used in jewelry, electronics, and dentistry, but more than half the gold mined is buried again—in bank vaults, as investments.

South Africa
Traditional gold mines were labor intensive.

The Great Gold Rush
Prospectors flocked to pan gold in 19th-century California, the Yukon, Canada, and Australia.

Vein gold
Gold may occur in quartz veins. It is extracted by crushing the ore for a concentrate, which is then smelted.

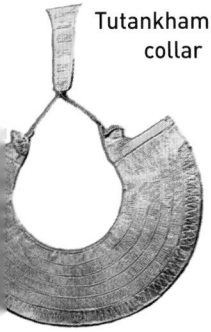

Tutankhamun's collar

Gold grains
Gold is also produced by smelting particles that have been dredged or panned then separated out from gravel and sand deposits.

Egyptian craft
The ancient Egyptians were one of the first civilizations to master the art of goldsmithing, using solid, beaten gold. Today, copper and silver are often added to gold (measured in carats) to make it harder.

Crystalline chalcopyrite

Fool's gold
Pyrite and chalcopyrite's brassy color can be mistaken for gold. But chalcopyrite, the main ore of copper, is more greenish-yellow, more brittle, and harder than gold, although not as hard as pyrite.

Massive chalcopyrite

Pyrite
Pyrite mostly forms cubic crystals and is closer in color to "white gold" or electrum, an alloy of gold and silver, than to pure gold.

Crystalline pyrite

Massive pyrite

Cutting and polishing

The earliest gemstones were rubbed together to produce a smooth surface, which could then be engraved. Much later, professional craftsmen (lapidaries) became skilled at cutting precious stones to maximize their optical effect and size.

Grinding and polishing agates in a German workshop c. 1800

Cutting gems

When mined, gemstones often look dull. To create a desirable, sparkling gem, the lapidary must cut and polish it to enhance its natural qualities, allowing for any flaws within.

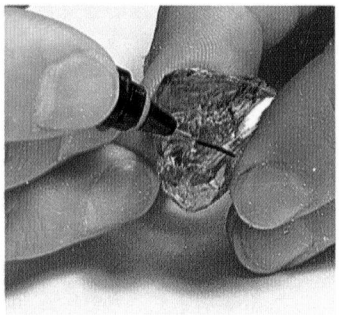

The hardest cut

Rough diamonds are marked with indian ink before cutting.

Popular cuts

The first, simple cuts included table and cabochon cuts. More complex, faceted cuts include the brilliant for diamond and other colorless stones.

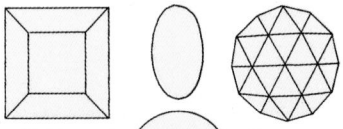

Table cut

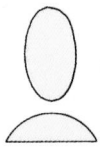

Cabochon

Rose cut

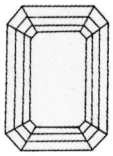

Emerald or step cut

Pear brilliant

Round brilliant

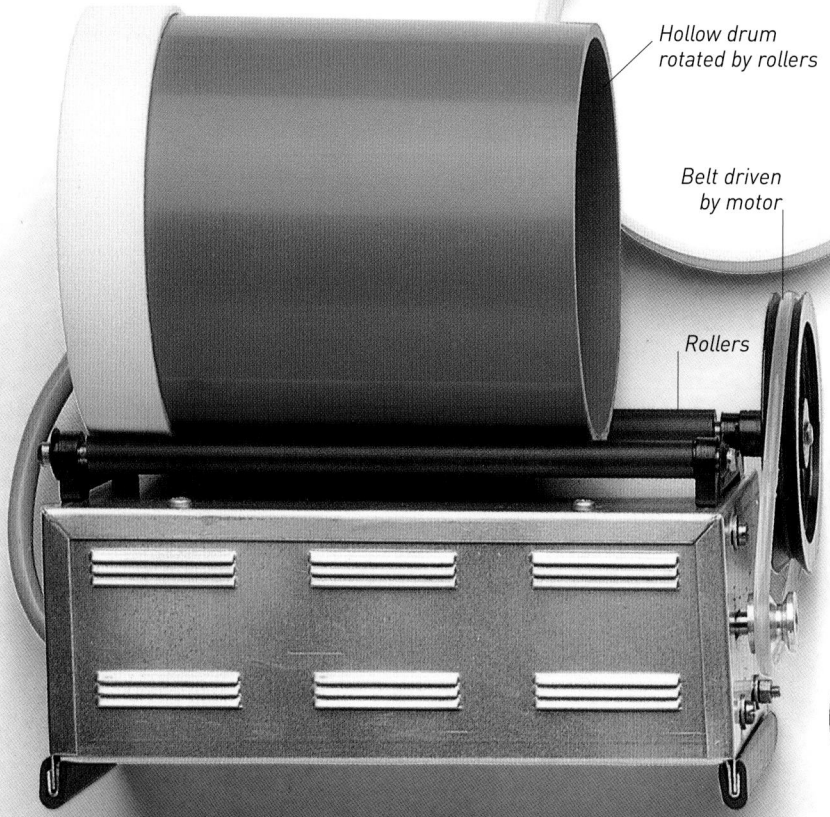

Lid of drum

Tumbling

Amateur lapidaries use a tumbling machine to rub pieces of mineral with coarse grit and water for about a week, then with finer grits until the pebbles are rounded and polished.

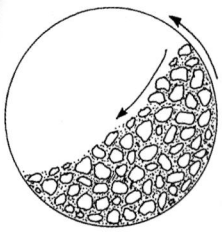

Tumbling action

As the drum rotates, pebbles are rubbed smooth and round.

Rough mineral pieces ready for tumbling

Grits and polishes

Grinding grits are used in sequence, from the coarsest to the finest.

Coarse grinding grit used in first tumbling

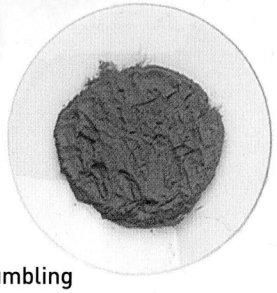

Fine grinding grit for second tumbling

Water added with grits

Cerium oxide, fine polishing powder finally makes pebbles smooth and sparkling

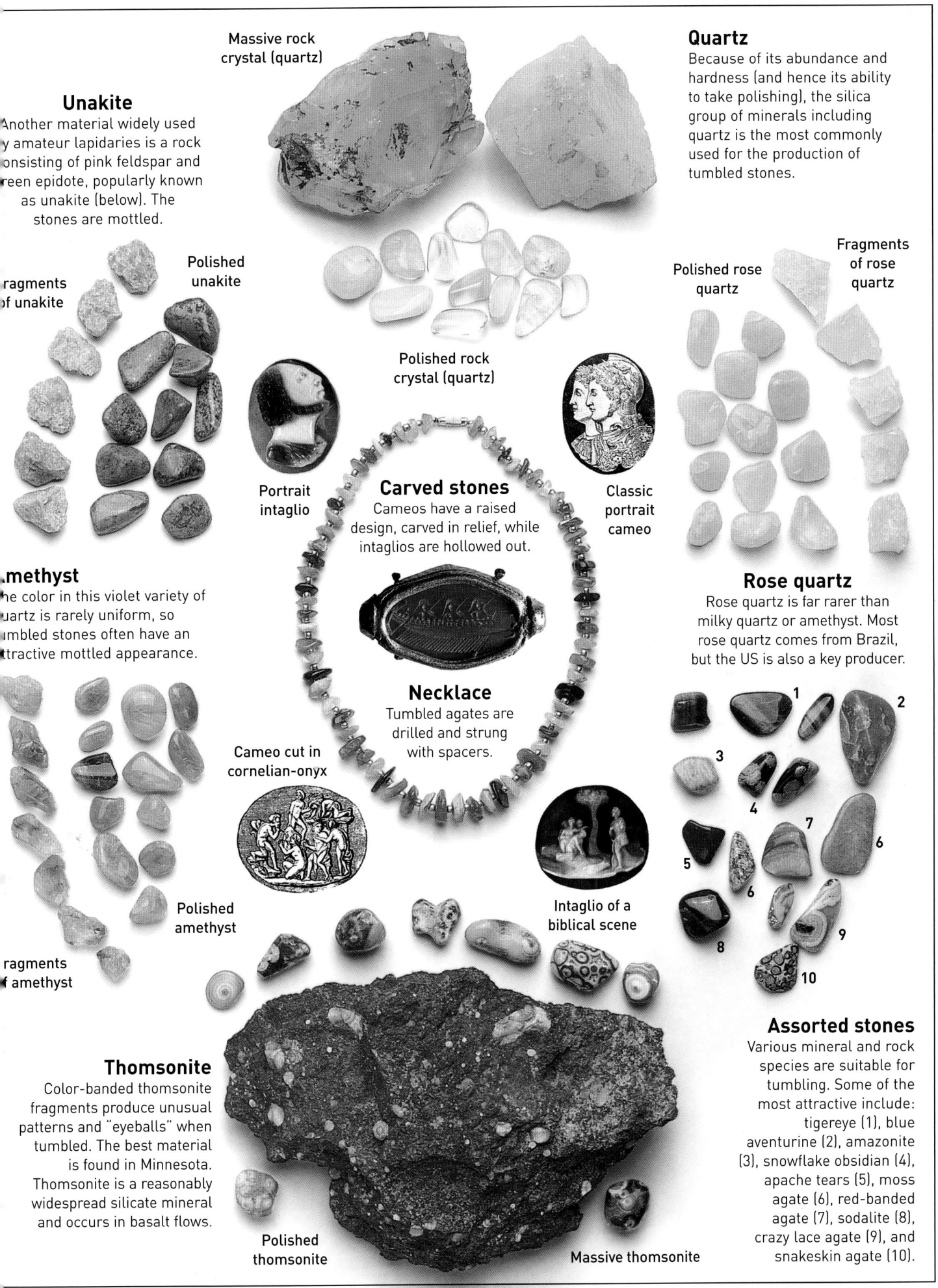
Massive rock crystal (quartz)
Quartz
Because of its abundance and hardness (and hence its ability to take polishing), the silica group of minerals including quartz is the most commonly used for the production of tumbled stones.
Unakite
Another material widely used by amateur lapidaries is a rock consisting of pink feldspar and green epidote, popularly known as unakite (below). The stones are mottled.
Polished unakite
Fragments of unakite
Polished rock crystal (quartz)
Polished rose quartz
Fragments of rose quartz
Portrait intaglio
Classic portrait cameo
Carved stones
Cameos have a raised design, carved in relief, while intaglios are hollowed out.
Amethyst
The color in this violet variety of quartz is rarely uniform, so tumbled stones often have an attractive mottled appearance.
Rose quartz
Rose quartz is far rarer than milky quartz or amethyst. Most rose quartz comes from Brazil, but the US is also a key producer.
Necklace
Tumbled agates are drilled and strung with spacers.
Cameo cut in cornelian-onyx
Intaglio of a biblical scene
Polished amethyst
Fragments of amethyst
1
2
3
4
5
6
7
8
9
10
Thomsonite
Color-banded thomsonite fragments produce unusual patterns and "eyeballs" when tumbled. The best material is found in Minnesota. Thomsonite is a reasonably widespread silicate mineral and occurs in basalt flows.
Assorted stones
Various mineral and rock species are suitable for tumbling. Some of the most attractive include: tigereye (1), blue aventurine (2), amazonite (3), snowflake obsidian (4), apache tears (5), moss agate (6), red-banded agate (7), sodalite (8), crazy lace agate (9), and snakeskin agate (10).
Polished thomsonite
Massive thomsonite

Starting a collection

Collecting mineral and rock specimens is a rewarding and popular pastime. It dates back to the amateur geologists of the 19th century, many of whom amassed impressive collections.

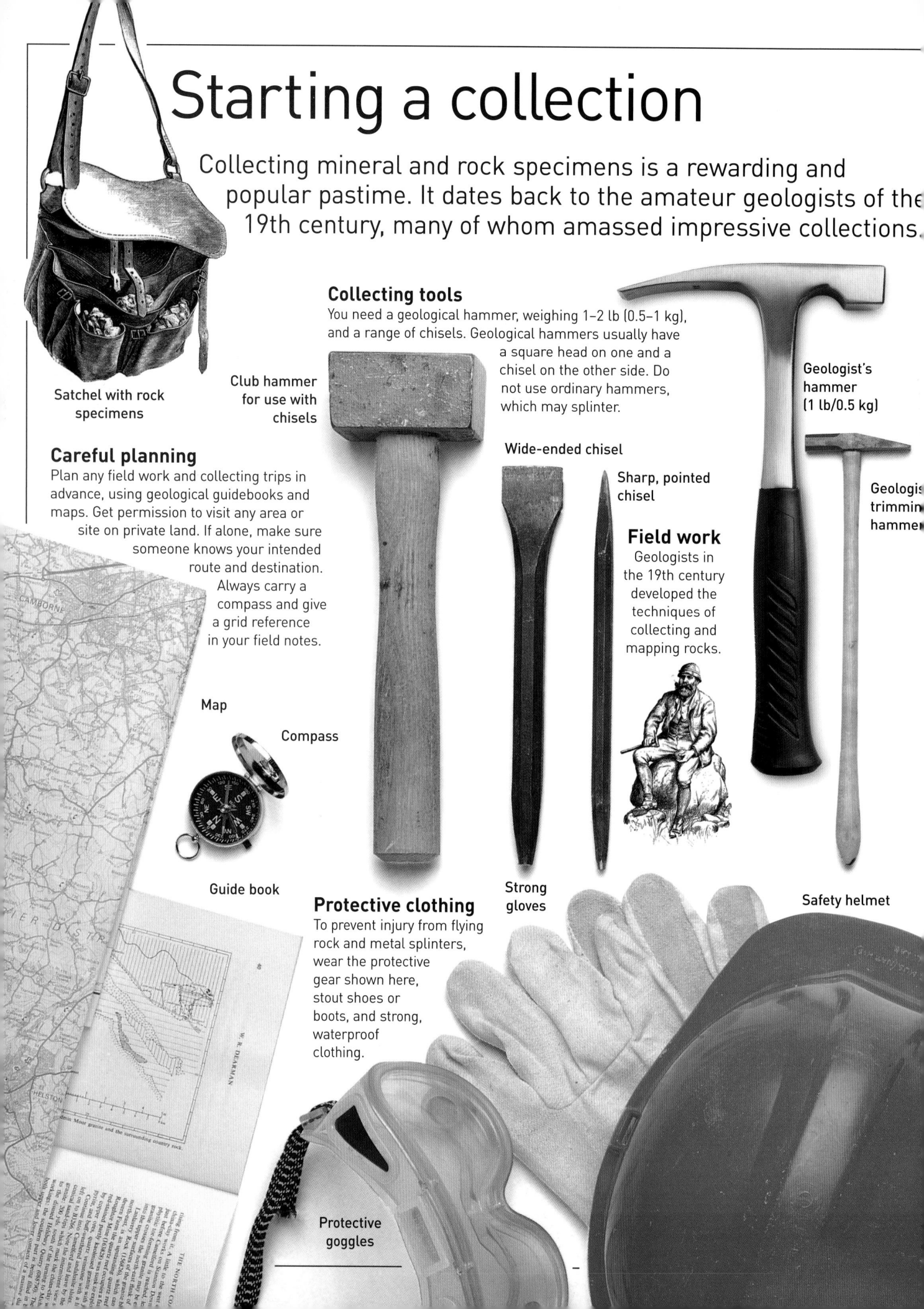

Satchel with rock specimens

Careful planning

Plan any field work and collecting trips in advance, using geological guidebooks and maps. Get permission to visit any area or site on private land. If alone, make sure someone knows your intended route and destination. Always carry a compass and give a grid reference in your field notes.

Map

Compass

Guide book

Collecting tools

You need a geological hammer, weighing 1–2 lb (0.5–1 kg), and a range of chisels. Geological hammers usually have a square head on one and a chisel on the other side. Do not use ordinary hammers, which may splinter.

Club hammer for use with chisels

Wide-ended chisel

Sharp, pointed chisel

Geologist's hammer (1 lb/0.5 kg)

Geologis trimmin hammer

Field work

Geologists in the 19th century developed the techniques of collecting and mapping rocks.

Protective clothing

To prevent injury from flying rock and metal splinters, wear the protective gear shown here, stout shoes or boots, and strong, waterproof clothing.

Strong gloves

Safety helmet

Warning

When rock-collecting, there are certain rules you should follow at all times: Always obey local laws, ask permission before entering private land, do not disturb wildlife, wear suitable clothing, use proper equipment, and make sure not to create hazards for others.

Recording a find

Number the specimen with a pen or tape and record the exact locality and details in a notebook, with a photo or sketch.

Notebook

Pencil

Pen

Identification

In the field, use a 10 magnification hand lens. Indoors, binocular microscope will reveal finer details.

Camera to record site or location of find—when taking photographs, try to include something to show scale

Spatulas for fine work, such as cutting around fossils

Surgical knife for fine preparatory work on fossils

Palette knife for extracting small crystals from soft fossils

Transporting

Wrap each specimen individually to prevent chipping or scratching. Since crystal groups are usually very fragile, pack them in tubes or boxes with wrapping and carry in collecting bags.

Sample bag

Newspaper

Plastic tube

Bubble wrap

Sealable plastic bag

Fine work

To remove surplus rock from a specimen, wash in water and scrub lightly with a soft brush. Or sift crumbly rock like clay for small crystals and bits of rock.

Trowel for digging soft rocks

Sieve for sorting material

Paintbrushes for cleaning specimens

Curating your collection

To prevent damage to specimens, store in individual trays or boxes in shallow drawers. Bear in mind their individual needs—some minerals deteriorate in damp, heat, or light.

Boxes for storing specimens

Labels for documenting specimens

Did you know?

AMAZING FACTS

After astronauts returned from the Moon, scientists discovered that the most common type of lunar rock is a basalt also found on Earth.

Spider fossilized in amber

Amber formed when sticky resin oozed from trees millions of years ago, sometimes trapping insects before it hardened.

The deeper into the crust a tunnel goes, the hotter it becomes. The deepest gold mines in South Africa have to be cooled down artificially so that people are able to work in them.

Devil's Tower, Wyoming

Devil's Tower, in Wyoming is a huge rock pillar made from lava that crystallized inside the vent of a volcano. Over thousands of years, the softer rock of the volcano itself has worn away.

More than 75 percent of the Earth's crust is made of silicates, minerals that are composed of silicon, oxygen, and some metals.

On some coastlines made up of soft rocks, the sea carves away yards of land every year. Some villages, such as Dunwich in Suffolk, UK, have partly fallen into the sea as cliffs collapsed.

Ice can shatter rock. Granite, one of the hardest rocks, can be split by water in cracks expanding as it freezes. The combined weight and movement of a glacier (a river of ice) can hollow out a whole mountainside.

Unaware it was poisonous, women in ancient Rome used the mineral arsenic as a cosmetic to whiten their skin.

Graphite, used in pencils, is also used in nuclear power plants. Huge graphite rods help to control the speed of nuclear reactions in the reactor core.

Obsidian is a black, volcanic rock that is so shiny that it was used as a mirror in ancient times.

Obsidian

Rocks are constantly changed by erosion and forces deep inside the Earth. Water and wind have carved out this sandstone arch over millions of years.

Fossil of *Archaeopteryx*

In 1861, a quarryman discovered the fossil of a birdlike creature with feathers that lived 150 million years ago. *Archaeopteryx* may link prehistoric reptiles and today's birds.

Minerals don't just exist in rocks. Your bones are made of minerals, too!

Rock arch in Utah

QUESTIONS AND ANSWERS

Q What are the most common rocks in the Earth's crust?

A Volcanic rocks, such as basalt, are the most common crustal rocks. Basalt forms from the more fluid type of lava as it cools and hardens. It makes up the ocean floors, which cover 68 percent of Earth's surface.

Q How do we know that dinosaurs existed?

A Dinosaur bones and teeth have been found as fossils in rocks all over the world (as have other animals and plants). Even their footprints and dung have been preserved in rock.

Fossilized footprint of a dinosaur

Chinese nephrite dragon

Q What is jade, and why has it got more than one name?

A In 1863, this rock was found to be two different minerals, now called jadeite and nephrite.

Q Why are the pebbles on a beach so many different colors?

A Pebbles are made up of many types of rock, washed up from many places. Their colors show what kinds of minerals they contain.

Q If pumice is a rock, why does it can float on water?

A Pumice is hardened lava froth from volcanoes on land and under the sea. It is full of tiny air bubbles—the air trapped inside these bubbles makes pumice light enough to float on water.

Q What made the stripes on the desert rocks in Utah?

A The rocks are made of layers of sandstone. Over millions of years, hot days, cold nights, floods, and storms have worn away the softer layers of rock, creating stripes in the landscape.

Badlands, Utah

Q What are the oldest rocks on the planet?

A The oldest known rocks came from space as meteorites. This chondrite is 4.6 billion years old. The first rocks to form on Earth are only 4.2 billion years old.

Chondrite

Q Are there new any rocks forming on Earth?

A New rocks form all the time: some from layers of sediment, others from volcanic activity under water and on land. Rock is constantly recycled by heat, pressure, and erosion.

Q What is a desert rose made from and how did it form?

A Desert rose is made of gypsum. It formed when water quickly evaporated, leaving impurities that formed crystals shaped like petals.

Desert rose

Record Breakers

MOST VALUABLE METAL
Platinum is the most valuable metal, more valuable than gold.

BIGGEST GOLD NUGGET
The largest gold nugget on record weighed 156 lb 6 oz (70.9 kg)—as heavy as a man.

MOST VALUABLE RELIGIOUS ITEM
The Golden Buddha of Bangkok is made of 6.1 tons (5.5 metric tons) of solid gold.

HARDEST MINERAL
Diamond is the hardest known mineral and cannot be scratched by any other.

BIGGEST STALAGMITE
A stalagmite in Krasnohorska, Slovakia, is 103 ft (31.5 m) tall.

BIGGEST ROCK
Uluru (Ayer's Rock) in Australia is the biggest freestanding rock in the world. It is 2¼ miles (3.6 km) long.

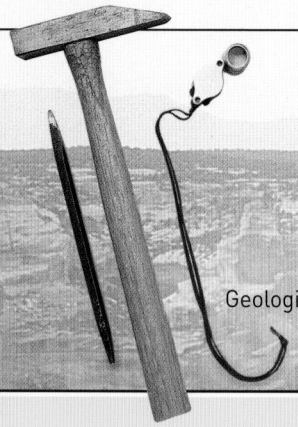

Geologist's tools

Rock or mineral?

Geologists classify rocks according to the way in which they were formed, in three main types: igneous, metamorphic, and sedimentary rocks.

IDENTIFYING ROCKS

Igneous rocks

Igneous rocks are made from hot, molten rock from deep within the Earth that has solidified as it has cooled. The more slowly a rock has cooled and solidified, the larger the crystals that have formed within it.

Large crystals of quartz, feldspar, and mica formed as the rock slowly cooled

Granite

Large crystals sthat formed as the rock cooled

Gabbro

Dark, fine-grained volcanic rock that formed from lava

Basalt

Glassy volcanic rock that cooled too quickly to form crystals

Obsidian

Metamorphic rocks

New metamorphic rocks form when sedimentary, igneous, or existing metamorphic rocks are transformed by heat and pressure in Earth's crust. The degree of heat is reflected by the size of crystals the minerals form.

Crinkled layers

Folded schist

Fine grain size

Slate

Dark and light bands of color

Gneiss

Sedimentary rocks

Sedimentary rocks are usually made from particles weathered and eroded from other rocks. The particles, from sand grains to boulders, are deposited in layers (strata) and slowly become rocks. These rocks can contain fossils.

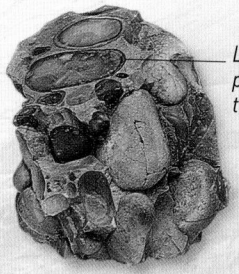

Large, coarse pebbles cemented together

Conglomerate

Iron oxide produces orange color

Sandstone

Angular fragments of rock held together by a fine, sandy material

Breccia

Formed from the skeletons of micro-organisms, chalk has a soft, powdery texture

Chalk

IDENTIFYING MINERALS

No two minerals are the same, and many have a color or shape that will help identify them. Some form large crystals; others form bubbly masses or grow as crusts on rocks.

Quartz
One of the most common minerals, quartz occurs in many rocks, often in mineral veins with metal ores. Quartz crystals usually have six sides with a top shaped like a pyramid.

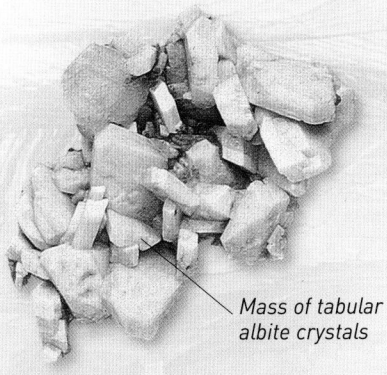

Albite
Usually white or colorless, albite is an important variety of feldspar, a rock-forming mineral, and is often found in granites, schists, and sandstones.

Calcite
The main mineral in limestone, which usually forms in a marine environment, calcite is also found in bone and shell, and makes stalactites and stalagmites.

Gold
Gold is a precious metal and a rare native element. Usually found as yellow specks in rocks, it often grows with quartz in mineral veins. Occasionally gold forms large crystalline nuggets.

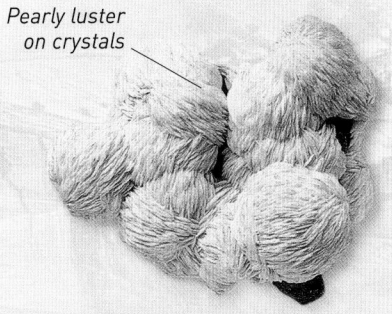

Cockscomb barite
Barite forms in many environments, from hot volcanic springs to mineral veins. Cockscomb barite is made up of rounded masses of soft, pearly crystals.

Sulfur
A native element, sulfur crystallizes around hot springs and volcanic craters, as a powdery crust of small crystals or as large crystals. Pure crystals are always yellow and soft.

Beryl
Formed deep in the crust, beryl is found mainly in granites and pegmatites. Transparent beryl is a rare and valuable gemstone—emerald and aquamarine are the best-known varieties.

Corundum
The pure form of corundum is colorless, but it comes in many colors—rubies and sapphires are two rare forms, mostly found in river gravels. Corundum is extremely hard.

Halite
Best known as rock salt, halite is one of the minerals called evaporites, which form when salty water evaporates. It is found in masses and as cubic crystals, around seas and lakes in dry climates.

Find out more

Rocks are all around you, on the ground and in walls, buildings, and sculptures. The best way to find out more about them is to collect them. Going on a trip or vacation ca also provide a chance to find different rock and discover new types of landscape. Here you will find suggestions for extensive museum collections and other good places to visit, as well as a list of useful websites.

Collecting pebbles
Pebble beaches, lakesides, and riverbanks are good places to look for specimens. See how many colors and types you can find. Always be careful near water.

Gathering information
Visit your local natural history or geological museum to see rocks and minerals, rare and common. Many museums also have displays on volcanoes, earthquakes, and rocks from space.

Earth L

Identifying specimens
You can take rock samples to some museums for help in identifying them. T Earth Lab at the Natural History Museu in London has 2,000 specimens of rocks minerals, and fossils, plus microscopes qualified advisers, and an online data si

Displaying your collection
Gently clean your rock samples with water and let them dry, then arrang them in empty matchboxes or small cardboard trays. For delicate items, line the trays with tissue paper. Put a small data card in the base of each tray, with the specimen's name, where you found it, and when.

PLACES TO VISIT

The following are some of the best natural history museums in the United States.

- **AMERICAN MUSEUM OF NATURAL HISTORY, NEW YORK, NEW YORK**
- **NATIONAL MUSEUM OF NATURAL HISTORY, SMITHSONIAN INSTITUTION WASHINGTON, D.C.**
- **CALIFORNIA MINING AND MINERAL MUSEUM, MARIPOSA, CALIFORNIA**
- **THE FIELD MUSEUM CHICAGO, ILLINOIS**

USEFUL WEBSITES

- A searchable guide to gemstones and minerals that offers photos, a glossary, and resources: **www.minerals.net**
- Find how rocks and minerals form and how to collect and identify rocks and minerals: **www.rocksforkids.com**
- The Minerology Database contains information on over 4,000 minerals, grouped by property: **www.webmineral.com**

Gemstones and jewelry

A good place to look for jewelry and other objects carved from rock is at a museum that features decorative arts, such as The Metropolitan Meseum of Art in New York.

Aztec jade necklace

he Grand Canyon

History in the rocks

The Grand Canyon, in Arizona, gives visitors a superb view of different layers of Earth's rocks. The canyon was carved out by the Colorado River over several million years. The rocks are mostly sandstones and limestones, and they contain bands of fossils from different geological periods. Going down the steep trails to the bottom is like traveling back in time.

Sculptures

Ancient Greeks and Romans used marble for fine statues and buildings. Look at statues closely to see if they are made from marble or another stone.

Marble statue of Pieta, St. Patrick's Cathedral, New York

Cave at Melissani, Cephalonia, Greece

Giant's steps

At the Giant's Causeway in Northern Ireland visitors can see hexagonal columns of rock up to 7 ft (2 m) tall. Legends says a giant built them as stepping-stones across the sea. In fact, they formed when basalt lava cooled and shrank.

imestone caves and grottos

imestone caves are good places to see stalactites. There are blue rottos on Mediterranean islands, such as Cephalonia and Malta. he Lascaux Caves in France have prehistoric cave paintings.

Glossary

ABRASION Erosion caused by water, wind, or ice laden with sediments, and scraping or rubbing against the surface of rocks.

ACICULAR Having a needlelike form.

ALLOY A metallic material, such as brass, bronze, or steel, that is a mixture of two types of metal.

CABOCHON A gemstone cut in which the stone has a smooth, domed upper surface without any facets.

CARAT The standard measure of weight for precious stones. One metric carat equals 0.2 g (0.007oz). Also used to describe the purity of gold; pure gold is 24 carat.

CLEAVAGE The way a crystal splits apart along certain well-defined planes according to its internal structure.

CORE The area of iron and nickel that makes up the center of the Earth. It is about 850 miles (1,370 km) in diameter.

CRUST The thin outer layer of the Earth. It varies in thickness between 4 and 43 miles (7 and 70 km).

Group of natural crystals

CRYSTAL A naturally occurring solid with a regular internal structure and smooth external faces.

DENDRITIC Having a branchlike form.

DEPOSIT A buildup of sediments.

ELEMENT One of the basic substances from which all matter is made. An element cannot be broken down into a simpler substance.

EROSION The wearing away of rocks on the Earth's surface by gravity, wind, water, and ice.

Ground worn away by erosion

EVAPORITE Mineral or rock formed as a result of salt or spring water evaporating.

EXTRUSIVE ROCK Formed when magma erupts as lava, which cools at the surface.

FACE A surface of a crystal.

FACET One side of a cut gemstone.

FIRE In gemstones, dispersed light. A gem with strong fire, like a diamond, is very bright.

FOSSIL The remains or traces of plants or animals preserved in Earth's crust, in rock, amber, permafrost, or tar.

Ammonite fossil

GALVANIZATION A process that adds zince to other metals or alloys to prevent them from rusting.

GEMSTONE Naturally occurring minerals, usually in crystal form, that are valued for beauty, rarity, and hardness.

GEOLOGIST A person who studies rocks and minerals to find out the structure of Earth's crust and how it formed.

Diamond

Sapphire

HABIT The shape and general appearance of a crystal or group of crystals.

INTRUSIVE ROCKS Igneous rocks that solidify within Earth's crust and only appear at the surface once the rocks lying on top of them have eroded away.

IRIDESCENCE A rainbowlike play of colors on the surface of a mineral, similar to that of a film of oil on water.

KARST SCENERY The broken rock formations of some limestone plateaus.

LAPIDARY A professional gem cutter.

LAVA Red-hot, molten rock (magma) from deep within the Earth that erupts on to the surface in volcanoes and other vents.

LUSTER The way in which a mineral shines. It is affected by how light is reflected from the surface of the mineral.

MAGMA Molten rock below the Earth's surface.

MANTLE The layer between Earth's core and crust. It is 1,800 miles (2,900 km) thick.

MASSIVE A term used to describe a mineral that has no definite shape.

MATRIX A mass of small grains surrounding large grains in a sedimentary rock.

METAMORPHOSE To undergo a change of structure. In rocks, this is usually caused by the action of heat or pressure.

METEORITE An object from space, such as a rock, that survives its passage through the atmosphere to reach Earth.

MINERAL A naturally occurring, inorganic solid with certain definite characteristics, such as crystal structure and chemical composition.

MINERAL VEIN A crack in rock filled by hot fluids' mineral deposits.

MOHS' SCALE A scale of hardness from 1 to 10 based on 10 minerals. Minerals of a higher number are able to scratch those of a lower number.

Meteorite

MOLTEN Melted, made into a liquid by great heat, especially rocks.

NATIVE ELEMENT An element that occurs naturally in a free state and does not form part of a compound.

NODULE A rounded lump of mineral found in sedimentary rock.

OOLITH Small, rounded grains in limestones.

OPAQUE Material that does not let light pass through it.

OPTICAL PROPERTIES The various optical effects produced as light passes through minerals. This is one of the properties used to help identify minerals.

ORE A rock or mineral deposit that is rich enough in metal or gemstone for it to be worth extracting.

OUTCROP The area that one type of rock covers on a geological map, including the parts covered by soil or buildings.

PALEONTOLOGIST A scientist who studies fossils.

PIGMENT A natural coloring material often used in paints and dyes. Many pigments were first made by crushing colored rocks and mixing the powders with animal fats.

POROUS Able to absorb water, air, or other fluids.

PORPHYRY An igneous rock containing fairly large crystals set into a finer matrix.

PRECIPITATION A chemical process during which a solid substance, such as lime, is deposited from a solution, such as lime-rich water.

Azurite, once ground into a prized blue pigment

PYROCLASTIC ROCK Pyroclastic means "fire-broken" and describes all the fragments of rock, pumice, and solid lava that may be exploded out of a volcano.

RESIN A sticky substance that comes from some plants and may harden to form amber, valued as a gem.

ROCK An aggregate of mineral particles.

Stalactites hanging from the roof of a cave

SEDIMENT Rock material of various sizes, ranging from boulders to silt, which is the product of weathering and erosion, as well as shell fragments and other organic material.

SMELTING The process of melting ore to extract the metal that it contains.

SPECIFIC GRAVITY A property defined by comparing the weight of a mineral with the weight of an equal volume of water.

STALACTITE A hanging spike made of calcium carbonate (lime) formed as dripping water precipitates lime from the roof of a cave. Over a long period of time, stony stalactites build up in size and may hang many feet from a cave roof.

STALAGMITE A stony spike standing on the base of a limestone cave. Stalagmites form where water has dripped from the roof of the cave or a stalactite above, slowly building up lime deposits.

STREAK The color produced when a mineral is crushed into a fine powder. The color of a streak is used to help identify minerals. It is often a better means of identification than the color of the mineral itself, since it is less variable.

STRIATIONS Parallel scratches, grooves, or lines on a crystal face that develop as the crystal grows.

SWALLOW HOLE A hollow in the ground, especially in limestone, where a surface stream disappears from sight and flows underground.

TRANSLUCENT Material that allows some light to pass through it, but is not clear.

TRANSPARENT Material that allows light to pass through it. It can be seen through.

TUMBLING The process of rolling rough mineral pieces in a tumbling machine with water and gradated sizes of grit until the pebbles are rounded and polished.

VEIN A deposit of foreign minerals within a rock fracture or a joint.

VESICLE A gas bubble or cavity in lava that is left as a hole after the lava has cooled and solidified.

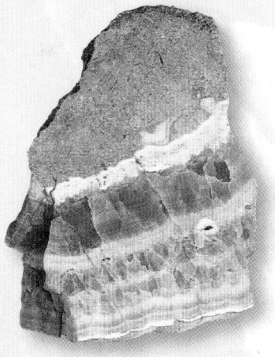

Veins of calcite

VOLCANIC BOMB A blob of lava that is thrown out of a volcano and solidifies before hitting the ground.

VOLCANIC VENT The central passage in a volcano, or a narrow fissure in the ground or on the seafloor through which magma flows and erupts as lava.

WEATHERING The breaking down of rocks on the Earth's surface. This is mainly a chemical reaction, aided by the presence of water, but it may also be due to processes such as alternate freezing and thawing, or to mechanical weathering by sediment-laden wind or ice.

Index

AB

acid lavas 18, 19
agate 52, 53, 60, 61
agglomerates 18
albite 43, 67
aluminum 42, 56
amber 14, 64
amethyst 55, 61
ammonites 20, 39
amphiboles 42
anthracite 7, 37
apatite 49
aquamarine 50, 67
arsenic 33, 64
asteroids 41
augite 8, 17, 43
azurite, 33, 45
barite 67
baryte 48
basalt 8, 9, 10, 16, 17, 19, 43, 64, 65, 66, 69
basic lavas 18, 19
bauxite 13, 56
beaches 65, 68
beryl 45, 46, 50, 67
biotite 8, 16, 25, 42
Black Prince's Ruby 54
bone 64, 67
bornite 56
breccia 18, 21, 27, 66
bricks 15, 35
building stones 34–35

CD

calcite 9, 17, 20, 22–23, 24, 42, 43, 45, 47, 48, 49, 67
cameos 53, 61
carbon 24, 37, 41, 48
carbonates 43
Carrara marble, 26
cassiterite, 6, 57
cave paintings, 32
caves, limestone, 22–23, 69
cement, 35
chalcanthite, 9
chalcedony, 42, 52–53
chalcopyrite 32, 46, 47, 56, 59
chalk 15, 20, 31, 32, 66
charcoal 32
chemical weathering 13
chondrite 65
cinnabar 32, 33, 57
citrine 6
clays 11, 21, 32, 35, 43
claystone 9, 11
cleavage 48
coal 7, 36–37
coastal erosion 64
collecting 62–63, 68
color, pigments 32
conglomerate 21, 31, 66
copper 27, 33, 56
core, Earth's 6
corundum 45, 47, 54, 67
crust, Earth's 6, 42, 64, 65
crystals 6, 44–47, 66, 67
cutting gemstones 60–61
desert rose 65
deserts 11, 12
diamonds 6, 48, 49, 50, 60, 65
dinosaurs 65
diorite 30, 42
dreikanters 12

EF

Earth, structure 6, 64, 65
Ease Gill Caves 22
eclogite 25
emeralds 50, 67
Empire State Building 35
erosion 12–13, 64
evaporites 7, 21, 67
extrusive rocks 16, 17
feldspars 8, 10, 13, 16–17, 24, 41, 42, 66, 67
feldspathoids 43
flint 15, 20, 21
tools, 28–29
fluorite 49
formation of rocks 10–11
fossils 6, 34, 38–39, 64, 65, 66

GH

gabbro 10, 17, 43, 66
galena 48, 49, 57
garnet 24, 25, 46, 55
gemstones 6, 50–55, 60–61, 69
Giant's Causeway 16, 17, 69
glaciers 13, 64
gneiss 10, 11, 25, 66
gold 6, 58, 59, 64, 65, 67
goniometer 45
Grand Canyon 21, 69
granite 7, 8, 10, 13, 15, 16, 30, 35, 42, 64, 66, 67
graphite 48, 64
Great Wall of China 35
grit 21
gypsum 21, 45, 49, 65
habits, crystal 46–47
halite 21, 47, 67
Halley's Comet 41
hardness 49
hematite 32, 33, 46, 56
hornblende 42
hornfels 24

IJK

ice 13, 64
identifying rocks and minerals 49, 66–67
igneous rocks 7, 8, 9, 10, 16–17, 42, 66
intaglios 61
intrusive rocks 10, 16
iron 42, 56
meteorites, 40, 41
jade 52, 53, 65, 69
jadeite 53, 65
jet 36
kaolin 32, 43
karst scenery 23
Kilimanjaro, Mount 7
kimberlite 6, 50
Koh-i-noor 50

LM

labradorite 8
lapis lazuli 33, 52
lava 7, 9, 10, 16, 17, 18–19, 64, 65, 66, 69
lead 31, 48, 57
lignite 37
limestone 6, 7, 13, 20, 24, 34–35, 39, 64, 67
caves 22–23, 69
pavements 22
magma 6, 7, 10, 16, 18
magnetism 49
magnetite 15, 49
malachite 33
man-made building stones 35
mantle, Earth's 6, 10
marble 24, 26–27, 69
Mars 41
mercury 57
metals 56–59, 67
precious, 6, 58–9
metamorphic rocks 10, 11, 24–25, 66
meteorites 40–41, 64, 65
mica 8, 11, 14, 24, 25, 42, 46, 49, 66
migmatites 10, 25
Mississippi River 11
Mohs' scale 49
Monument Valley 12
Moon rocks 41, 64
mountain-building 6, 24

NO

nephrite 53, 65
nickel 57
Nile River 7
nodules 9, 14, 15
norite 9
Notre Dame 35
nuclear reactors 64
obsidian 16, 19, 29, 64, 66
ocean floors 65
oil shale 36
olivine 8, 9, 15, 17, 19, 40, 43, 45, 54
onion-skin weathering 12
oolitic limestone 20, 34
opals 42, 51
optical properties 49
ore minerals 6, 56–57
orpiment 32, 33
orthoclase 8, 42, 45, 49

PQ

Pamukkale Falls 23
Parthenon 13
peat 36, 37
pebbles 6, 14–15, 30, 65, 68
Pelée, Mount 9
Pele's hair 9
pegmatite 67
peridot 8, 54
peridotite 17
pigments 32–33
pitchstone 16
plagioclase feldspar 8, 9, 17, 43
platinum 6, 58, 65
plutonic *see* intrusive rocks
Pompeii 19
porphyry 17
Portland stone 34
precious metals 6, 58–59
properties of minerals 48–49
pumice 19, 65
Puy de Dôme 10
pyramids 34
pyrite 6, 14, 45, 47, 59
pyroclastic rocks 18
pyroxene 8, 9, 17, 19, 24, 25, 40, 41, 43
pyrrhotite 49
quartz 8, 16, 24, 42, 59, 66, 67
crystals 6, 44, 45, 47
formation 11
pebbles 15
polishing 61
properties 48, 49
sand 14
quartzite 11, 24, 30

RS

realgar 33
rhyolite 19, 30
rivers 7, 11, 50
rock crystal 42, 44, 61, 67
rock salt 21, 67
ropy lavas 7, 19
rose quartz 61
rubies 51, 67
rutile 56
St. Helens, Mount 18
salt 21, 47, 67
sand 11, 12, 14–15, 47, 65
sandstone 11, 12, 14, 21, 35, 64, 65, 66
sapphires 51, 67
schists 10, 11, 24, 25, 66
seashores 14–15, 64, 65
sedimentary rocks 7, 9, 11, 14, 20–21, 38, 66
sediments 12, 13, 20, 38
serpentinite 17
shale 21, 25
shells 6, 14, 20, 38–39, 67
siderite 45
silica 20, 42
silicates 64
silver 6, 58
slate 14, 24, 25, 34, 66
specific gravity 49
sperrylite 58
sphalerite 47, 57
spinels 54
stalactites 9, 22, 23, 67, 69
stalagmites 22, 23, 65, 67
stibnite 48
structure, Earth's 6
Sugar Loaf Mountain, 10
sulfur 67
swallow holes 22
symmetry, crystal 45

T

Taj Mahal 27
talc 49
temperature, weathering 12
thomsonite 61
till 13
tin 6, 56, 57
titanium 56
tools 28–31, 62–63
topaz 49, 54
tors 13
tourmaline 32, 45, 55
travertine 23
tremolite 42, 46
tufa 21, 22
tuff 18, 30
tumbling 60–61
turquoise 52
twin crystals 45

UVWZ

unakite 61
vesicular volcanic rocks 17
Vesuvius 19
volcanic ash 15, 18, 21
volcanic rocks 7, 17, 18–19, 64, 65, 66
volcanoes 9, 10, 18–19, 64, 65
weathering 6, 10, 11, 12–13
whetstones 31
wind erosion 12
wulfenite 9, 45
zinc 57
zircon 45, 54

Acknowledgments

Dorling Kindersley would like to thank: Dr. Wendy Kirk of University College London; the staff of the British Museum (Natural History); Gavin Morgan, Nick Merryman, & Christine Jones at the Museum of London for their advice & invaluable help in providing specimens; Redland Brick Company & Jacobson Hirsch for the loan of equipment; Anne-marie Bulat for her work on the initial stages of the book; David Nixon for design assistance; Tim Hammond for editorial assistance; Fred Ford & Mike Pilley of Radius Graphics, and Ray Owen & Nick Madren for artwork.

For this relaunch edition, the publisher would also like to thank: Camilla Hallinan for text editing and Carron Brown for proofreading

The publisher would like to thank the following for their kind permission to reproduce their images:
a=above, b=bottom, c=center, f=far, l=left, m=middle, r=right, t=top

Airbus-image exm company: P. Masclet 56bl. **Ardea London Ltd.:** Francois Gohier 65t. **Didier Barrault / Robert Harding Picture Library:** 37mr. **Bridgeman Art Library / Bonhoms, London:** 55mr. **Paul Brierley:** 49b; 51m. **British Museum (Natural History):** 42m; 43. **N. A. Callow / Robert Harding Picture Library:** 13b. **Bruce Coleman Ltd:** Derek Croucher 69br; Jeff Foott 65bl; Natural Selection Inc 64br. **G. & P. Corrigan / Robert Harding Picture Library:** 23t. **GeoScience Features Picture Library:** 68tr. **Diamond information Centre:** 60m. **C. M. Dixon / Photoresources:** 11b; 14t; 15t; 19b; 32b. **Earth Satellite Corporation / Science Photo Library:** 7t. **Mary Evans Picture Library:** 6t; 8; 9m; 12b; 15b; 16tl; 19t; 25; 26b; 28b; 30bl; 31b; 32t; 34t, ml; 36t; 37t, bl; 39b; 40t; 41t; 44tr; 50tr, br; 56mr; 57m; 58tl, tr; 59tl, b; 62t, m. **Clive Friend / Woodmansterne Ltd.:** 15m, 36b. **Jon Gardey / Robert Harding Picture Library:** 40b. **Geoscience Features:** 18t. **Mike Gray / University College London:** 17; 20tr; 24tf. **Ian Griffiths / Robert Harding Picture Library:** 13t. **Robert Harding Picture Library:** 13m; 18br; 21; 22bl; 23m; 27t, b; 35t, b; 56t; 59m. **Brian Hawkes / Robert Harding Picture Library:** 12m. **Michael Holford:** 50tl, bl; 51t; 54t, mr; 55t, ml. **Glenn I. Huss:** 40m. **The Hutchinson Library:** 35m; 51b; 56ml. **INAH:** Michel Zabé 69tr. **Yoram Lehmann/ Robert Harding Picture Library:** 37ml. **Kenneth Lucas / Planet Earth:** 39t. **Johnson Matthey:** 58bl. **Museum of London:** 28t; 32m; 61tl, br. **NASA:** 41br. **NASA/Robert Harding Picture Library:** 6–7, 7b. **NASA / Spectrum Color Library:** 11t. **National Coal Board:** 37br. **The Natural History Museum, London:** 68cl, 68cr, 71crb. **N.H.P.A.:** Kevin Schafer 64cl. **Walter Rawlings / Robert Harding Picture Library:** 26m; 33b. **John G. Ross/Robert Harding Picture Library:** 53. **K. Scholz / ZEFA:** 10b. **Nicholas Servian / Woodmansterne:** 34mr. **Silva:** 62crb. **A. Sorrell / Museum of London:** 29t. **Science Photo Library:** Charles D. Winters: jacket, b. **Spectrum Color Library:** 10m. **R. F. Symes:** 9tr. **A. C. Waltham / Robert Harding Picture Library:** 22br. **Werner Forman Archive:** 29b; 30br; 31tl, ml; 52t, b, 55b; 61m. **G. M. Wilkins / Robert Harding Picture Library:** 47. **Woodmansterne:** 58br. **ZEFA:** 16tr. **Zeiss:** 41bl. **Reproduced with the premission of the Controller of Her Majesty's Stationery Office, Crown copyright:** 54ml. **Illustrations:** Andrew Macdonald 6m, b; 14ml; 18bl; 22ml; 28mr; 30mr.

All other images © Dorling Kindersley.
For further information, see:
www.dkimages.com